T5-ACX-544

Martin Hall's
Golf Myths Exposed

PGA TOUR PARTNERS CLUB

GAME IMPROVEMENT LIBRARY™

CREDITS

MARTIN HALL'S GOLF MYTHS EXPOSED

Copyright © 2003 PGA TOUR Partners Club

All rights reserved. No part of this publication may be reproduced, stored in an electronic retrieval system or transmitted in any form or by any means (electronic, mechanical, photocopying, recording or otherwise) without the prior written permission of the copyright owner.

Tom Carpenter
Creative Director

Heather Koshiol
Managing Editor, Book Development

Julie Cisler
Book Design & Production

Michele Teigen
Senior Book Development Coordinator

Steve Hosid
Instruction Editor/Photographer

Steve Ellis
Editor

Ward Clayton **Leo McCullagh**
Bob Combs **Mike Mueller**
PGA TOUR

Special thanks to the following golf courses for allowing us to shoot on location:
Arnold Palmer's Bay Hill Club & Lodge: Orlando, Florida
Ibis Golf and Country Club: West Palm Beach, Florida
Hammock Creek: Palm City, Florida

Acknowledgements
"To the members of the PGA TOUR Partners Club I meet at tournaments around the country: Your questions, comments and support help create articles and books that truly reflect the needs of our outstanding membership."
—*Steve Hosid*

8 7 6 5 4 3 2 1 / 09 08 07 06 05 04 03
ISBN 1-58159-190-X
PGA TOUR Partners Club
12301 Whitewater Drive
Minnetonka, Minnesota 55343

ABOUT THE AUTHORS

Steve Hosid (left) and Martin Hall emphasize how the understanding of what the face of your club is doing will improve your game.

Martin Hall

Martin Hall has long been considered one of golf's top instructors and can be seen frequently on The Golf Channel's *Academy Live*. Martin also appears in the PGA TOUR Partners Club Instruction videos and in the Club's Game Improvement books. Martin is Director of Golf Instruction at Ibis Golf and Country Club located in West Palm Beach, Florida. He can be reached at 561-624-8922.

Steve Hosid

Steve Hosid is also instruction editor and photographer for *PGA TOUR Partners* magazine and writer and photographer for the Club's Game Improvement Library. Steve has written 15 books, 10 of which are on golf and feature the game's top stars. He can be heard weekly on several radio shows broadcast around the country.

Contents

Introduction   *4*
Golf's Real Truths   *6*
Garden Chat   *8*

SECTION I
ELIMINATING THE MYTHS   12

CHAPTER 1
TOP TEN MISLEADING TERMS AND ANALYSES   14
Myth #1: Keep the Left Arm Straight   16
Myth #2: Keep the Clubhead Low to the Ground   18
Myth #3: Turn, Turn, Turn   22
Myth #4: Keep Your Head Down   26
Myth #5: Swing Back Straight   28
Myth #6: Extension   30
Myth #7: Weight Shift   33
Myth #8: Swing Inside to Outside   35
Myth #9: You're Swinging Over the Top   38
Myth #10: Trapped Behind   40

CHAPTER 2
WHY AREN'T YOU PLAYING BETTER?   42
270 Degrees of Rotation   44
Move Within the Move   45
Slice-Producing Chain Reaction   48
Hook-Producing Chain Reaction   50

CHAPTER 3
INSTINCTS OR INTELLECT: WHICH IS IT?   52
Opposite Instincts   54
Symmetrical Swing Plane: The One and Only Truth   58
'Plane' Simple Geometry   60
Sweet Spot   62

SECTION II
VEGETABLES BEFORE DESSERT   64

CHAPTER 4
BUILDING A BALANCED GOLF SWING   66
Martin's Top Ten Hits   68
Grip   69
Ball Position   74
Ball Position Drill   76
Balanced Posture   77
Balanced Posture Drills   80
Dynamic Balance   84
Dynamic Balance Drill   85

CHAPTER 5
BACKSWING: ESTABLISHING GOLF'S BASIC GEOMETRY   86
Train/Golf Synergy   88
Backswing Drills   90
Backswing Coil Drills   98

CHAPTER 6
TRANSITION   106
The Balanced Transition   108
Transition Drills   110
Smooth Acceleration Drills   113

CHAPTER 7
DOWNSWING TO IMPACT   116
Goal: Solid Hits   118
Hit Impulse: A Rogues' Gallery   119
Impact Drills   120

CHAPTER 8
PAST IMPACT TO FINISH   128
Three Keys for Success   130
Clubhead Rotation   131
Clubhead Rotation Drill   132
Johnny Miller Recoil Drills   133
Past Impact to Finish Drills   136

SECTION III
TIME FOR DESSERT   138

CHAPTER 9
GOLF'S ONLY SECRET: SQUARE AT IMPACT   140
Important Swing Check Positions   142
Square at Impact Drills   144
Power Punch   146
Head on Pillow   147

CHAPTER 10
CHANGING FICTION TO FACTS   148
Curing a Slice   150
Changing Fiction to Facts Drills   152

Epilogue   *156*
Glossary   *157*
Index   *158*

INTRODUCTION

Over the years, most golfers have fallen prey to some bad or incomplete information that has led them unknowingly down the wrong path—the path away from true game improvement. In fact, if we could speed back in a time machine to the mid-1400s, when a golfer teed up the very first ball in a Scottish sheep meadow, we undoubtedly would find a well-meaning friend, hands on kilt, telling the first golfer to keep his head down.

These "helpful" individuals are harder to get rid of than ticks on a dog, and the distressing part is that their spiel sounds logical on the surface. Unfortunately, the information is often worse than just being wrong. It's harmful to your game's progress!

That's precisely why we created this book. As a member of the PGA TOUR Partners Club you take your game seriously, and constantly strive to improve. You rightly demand the best instruction and are willing to devote the time for practicing if you know it will yield the results you are striving for. You'll find all that here, with a bonus. As we debunk the myths and misconceptions, your newfound knowledge will serve as a shield to protect you from the golf know-it-alls. You will deflect the misinformation and concentrate only on what you know will truly improve your game.

Chapter 1 features the antithesis of the well-meaning purveyor of misleading advice, a character we call "Helpful Henry." In real life, he is fellow Partners Club member and prominent Orlando attorney Bob Jack. He looks the part (although we did dress him in some outlandish clothes), because the Helpful Henrys of this world are disguised as your closest golfing buddy or just a fellow range rat ready to throw a lifeline to a distressed friend. Actually their help is more like throwing you a line attached to a sinking anchor while you're treading water.

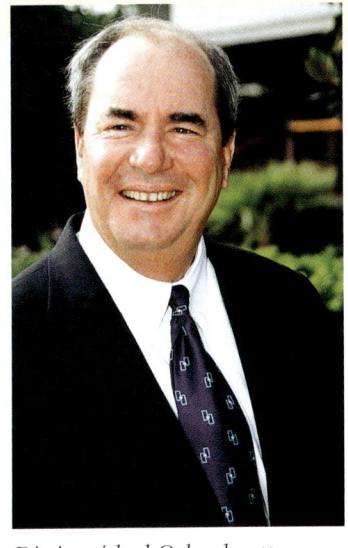

Distinguished Orlando attorney and Partners Club member Bob Jack portrays "Helpful Henry" in Chapter 1. Henry represents the guy we all know who doles out well-meaning but misleading golf swing information.

The rest of the book both helps you build a repeatable golf swing and shares some of the secrets of the pros. For instance, do you know that golf's *knockout blow* compresses the ball for maximum distance and accuracy?

This is a serious book for serious golfers. You will have lots of fun building a solid game with some very interesting drills that you can execute away from the course. Perfecting your swing mechanics at home allows you to concentrate on reaching your targets with confidence when you practice at the range … just like the pros.

And always remember—golf is a game, so enjoy it. Of course, the best way to increase the fun level is to play better. We know this book will boost you to higher levels of game improvement.

Martin Hall   Steve Hosid

Introduction

5

Golf's Real Truths
A Quick Reference for Playing Better Golf

Myths and misconceptions may have been holding back your game improvement progress. But here is the truth: 10 facts to really help you improve, along with Martin's knowledge, help and easy-to-do drills.

Truth #1: Square at Impact

The clubface should only be square to the target line at the moment of impact. The entire book is dedicated to helping you develop a golf swing that is capable of arriving in this correct position consistently. See especially Chapter 9.

Truth #2: Correct Grip Is Vital

Gripping the club correctly is the single most important thing any golfer can do to change the clubface position at impact. See page 69.

Truth #3: Maintain Your Natural Extension

Your genetics dictate the natural limit of your swing extension. Maintaining this natural extension helps the clubhead remain on plane. See page 93.

Truth #4: Correct Takeaway Swing Plane

Keeping the clubface looking at the ball for as long as possible develops the correct takeaway swing plane. See page 96.

Golf Myths Exposed

6

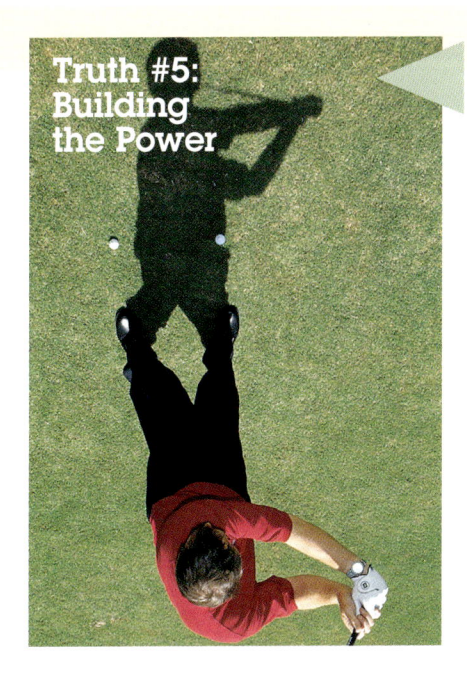

Truth #5: Building the Power

Your shadow shows if your coil is correct. See page 102.

Truth #6: Transition Like a Pro

Your lower body must lead the transition. See page 114.

Truth #7: A Key to Solid Hits

Solid hits come from compressing the ball at impact as a result of following the correct plane, with the hands slightly ahead. See page 118.

Truth #8: Positive Energy Release

Energy is transferred through the clubhead to the ball at the bottom of the swing arc. See page 124.

Truth #9: Five Times Parallel Keeps You on Plane

During the golf swing the shaft should be parallel to the target line 5 times. See page 143.

Truth #10: Golf's Power Punch

The left leg and right arm snap straight just after impact. See page 146.

Golf's Real Truths

7

Garden Chat

"Only when people really understand what it is they are trying to do, can they truly improve."
—Martin Hall

As the "King" himself loosened up on the nearby practice range, Martin Hall and coauthor Steve Hosid walked to "The Hummingbird Garden" at Arnold Palmer's Bay Hill Club & Lodge in Orlando, after completing this book's final photo shoot. The garden, a living memorial to Winnie Palmer, provided the perfect atmosphere to reflect on Martin's goals for this book. He elaborated on his passion for helping golfers of all levels improve. The keys to improvement? Eliminating costly myths and misconceptions that have been holding them back.

Having personally gone down that same wrong road while trying to improve his own game, Martin found the way back after discovering reliable information that held up to his scrutiny. As you will see in this garden chat, his personal experiences fuel a continuing drive for developing better and better methods for helping his students understand and master the golf swing.

Steve Hosid: Martin, golfers of all levels are always looking for the quick cure, the one thing that will send their games soaring to new levels. Does such a tip really exist?

Martin Hall: *Change what the clubface is doing!* It's not exactly a quick cure but it's the one and only cure. Everything you do from the moment you take your club out of the bag to the moment that ball has been hit should be to influence and improve how your clubface meets the ball. Golf shots are never awful; they are always *law*ful! The ball does exactly what it should do, what it can do, based on your clubface at impact.

Steve: Over the years I've watched you use dog leashes, bungie cords, brooms and buckets to help your students develop correct feelings for various parts of the swing.

Martin: Honestly, with every lesson I give I keep thinking, "Is there a better way to do this? How can I get the person I'm working with or the readers to hit balls better?" The objects you mentioned, along with many more, represent things people can relate to, and by using them in drills, I believe every golfer can play better. I'm not saying they will play better than Tiger Woods, but they can play better than they do now.

The great teacher Claude Harmon once said: "I may not be able to turn you into a thoroughbred, but I may be able to turn you into a racing mule!" Working on the right stuff, and not getting caught up in the misconceptions and myths, gives you the best chance for becoming a good player.

Steve: With so much instructional information available to golfers—magazines, TV broadcasts and so forth—why do so many golfers get caught up in the trap of following the wrong information and misinterpreting what they really should be doing in their swings?

Martin: I'm a good example of someone who used faulty information while trying to improve. When I was 15, I used to leak the ball a little left to right for a fade, and I hated that. In my group of friends, you weren't a man if you couldn't draw the ball. Regrettably, I later learned that I should have stayed with the fade, but back then it was a sissy thing to do.

When I was growing up in England, we didn't have *PGA TOUR Partners* magazine to rely on for accurate information, so I bought the hot magazine of the time featuring an instruction article that said, "If you want to draw the ball, you must swing from in to out." I went down this wrong road, suffering through an entire list of chain reactions that made things even worse. Trying to swing inside to outside resulted in whipping the club behind me too much on my backswing.

Misconceptions all share the same similarity: There is a grain of truth mixed in with the rubbish. In this case, feeling a swing going from in to out can be good, but the actual in-to-out swing is incorrect.

If I could have been my own teacher back then, I would have told myself, **"Don't you dare swing from in to out!** *Instead, strengthen the left hand grip and do something to change the clubface position."*

You do not need to go down a road making 64 changes per mile. Once you understand what the clubface does, it changes the swing quite quickly. But until you change what the clubface does, you change nothing.

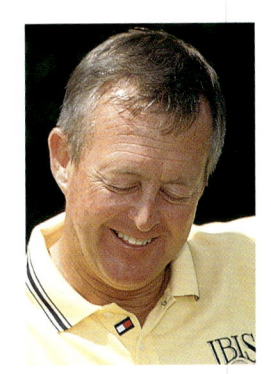

Steve: How do some of the more popular and damaging misconceptions and myths get started, and who perpetuates them?

Martin: There is plenty of blame to go around—like misunderstanding what a TV analyst is saying when his opinion may not correlate to the camera angle you're seeing. But one of the true perpetuators of this misinformation that spreads like a plague across the land can perhaps be found in your own Sunday morning foursome.

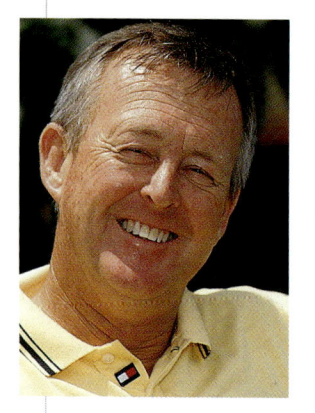

You know him. He's the guy who says *"You raised your head up"* when you hit a shot thin. He may have been at the hot dog cart at the time, not even looking at you, but he knows your problem! His other favorite is, *"You didn't keep your left arm straight."* But it doesn't stop with those two.

We'll be correcting that type of misinformation in this book. Myths often sound reasonable, but using the misinformation as the basis for working on your game sends it on an even steeper downward spiral.

Steve: We all know somebody like that. He's sort of like a racecourse tout whispering wrong information to you in what seems a knowledgeable sort of way. They seem to thrive on the practice range, and we give him a featured role throughout the book. We're calling him *Helpful Henry*.

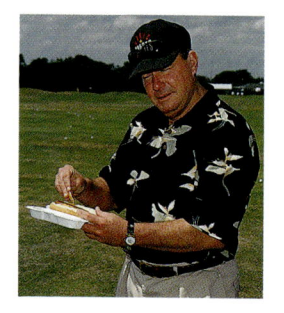

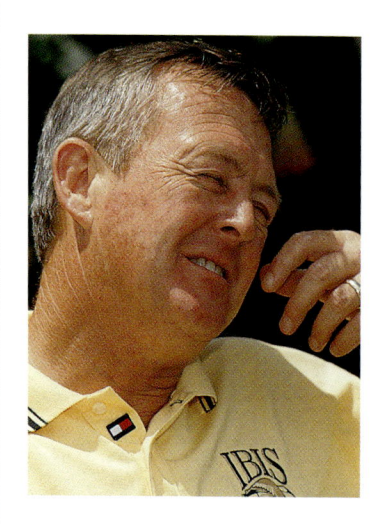

Martin: Helpful Henry illustrates the type of information to stay away from. The funniest phrase a teacher hears is when a 19-handicapper tells a 20-handicapper, "You know, I can't do it myself but I can see what you're doing wrong."

Again, like other misconceptions, there is a grain of truth to that, because a good teacher is not necessarily someone with the knowledge of how the gears and levers work, but is someone who can teach people how to hit the ball better.

Harvey Penick was a great example. While some people say that his teachings were lightweight, I disagree. They were brilliant because he could achieve so much by saying so little.

Steve: Your drills are brilliant and many of them are designed to be done away from the course and practice range.

Martin: It all has to do with the reality of how long it really takes for correct changes to infiltrate your system. Golf is not a simple sport, and it takes time to change. Many of these drills can be done away from the course, helping you to learn faster.

The style I've developed may use a shoe box, a shaft or dog leashes, beating a carpet with a broom, or some other such image. Images give people things they can practice at home to create muscle memory. Biologists may argue that muscle memory does not exist, so let's think of it in terms of your brain remembering how the muscles should move.

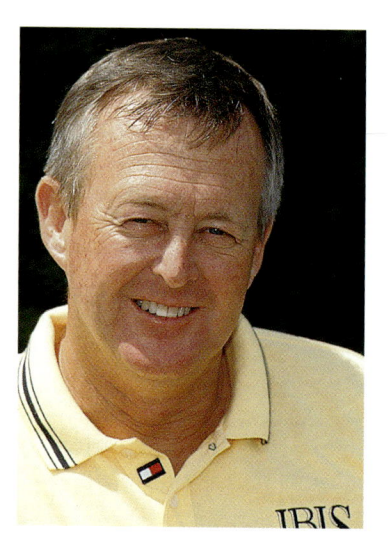

To change a habit using motor skills, you just can't think about it because real change takes about *twenty- to thirty-thousand correct repetitions.* Those are correct repetitions, not just shots hit before you own the new habit. That translates into hitting 600 balls correctly each week for a year. A hundred balls a day hit correctly for a year before you own the change! The TOUR pros hit many more than that.

Most amateur golfers can't devote that much time to improving at the course or practice range, so I developed drills you can do at home. Used together with drills designed for the range, this book helps you improve even in your spare time at home or while traveling. It keeps you constantly moving in the right direction along the road to better golf.

Steve: Martin, I know your reputation as one of the game's most respected instructors. *(Author's note: Martin is regularly listed among golf's top 100 instructors and garners some of the highest ratings when he appears on the Golf Channel's* Academy Live.*)* Did you ever play competitively?

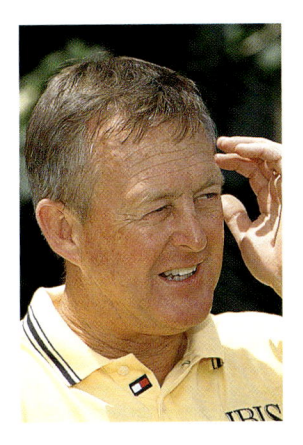

Martin: I started playing at 12 years old and fell in love with golf immediately. Some people find golf easy, but I didn't; and because of my determination to become a good player, I took lessons. As I look back, there was some truth to what I was told, but unfortunately many untruths as well.

I worked hard on my game, and by the time I was 15, my handicap was down to a one. It was at this point that I began reading and listening to tips, and coincidentally my game started going south.

But through all of this I made it to the European Tour at 20. My first tournament was the 1976 Portuguese Open. I remember watching Seve Ballesteros on the practice range and saying to myself, "I can't compete with this man." Watching Seve and the other better players made me realize they were doing something I wasn't. Now I wasn't exactly sure *what* that was at the time, but I watched them and learned.

I played for several years on the European Tour, but during one of the years when I lost my card, I turned to teaching golf.

Steve: How has your style of teaching evolved over the years? I doubt the Martin Hall we know today was the same instructor back then.

Martin: That's true because I wanted to teach, but to be honest, I didn't have an idea *what* to teach. I would pick up current issues of the golf magazines, and whatever their tip of the month was, that's what I would teach until the next issue came out.

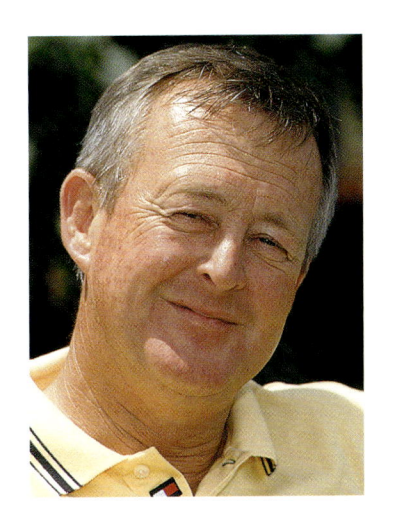

Steve: What was the turning point in your teaching career?

Martin: I asked one of my friends who was going to America to bring me back some golf instruction books. Now remember I had been going to some of the better known teachers in Europe, reading all sorts of books on golf, but it didn't make any sense to me. Something was missing.

With the books my friend bought back, it started to finally make sense. Bob Toski's book really piqued my interest with his different style. Toski's teaching technique dealt with the importance of grip pressure and the pace of the swing and especially the legs' role during the downswing. Later, I had a chance to attend a seminar Toski gave with Jim Flick and Peter Kostis in Europe, and forged a lifelong friendship with them.

Steve: What you're saying is that if a student and our readers really want to improve they should challenge and think their way through the material, not just accept it. They have to come to understand it and believe in it before they can really learn it.

Martin: That's exactly the point I'm trying to make based on my own experiences. You must truly understand something before you can master it. When I hear a student say "I understand what to do but I just can't do it" my response is along these lines: "Please don't take this the wrong way, but you only think you understand what to do, because if you really understood it, you would be able to do it."

So I challenge our readers in this book: Is the same thing true with your game? Do you really understand what you hear or read, well enough to improve the quality of your golf game?

My challenge is to provide you with correct information presented in such a way that you can relate to it and be able to master it using the simple practice drills. We want to show you what is appropriate for you to improve.

Section I
Eliminating the Myths

With all the misconceptions and myths floating around the practice ranges and golf courses these days, I'm surprised they don't enshroud players like fog on the moors. Everyone has a friend or knows someone like "Helpful Henry," this book's resident bearer of misinformation. In this section he spews out some harmful myths and misconceptions, but I won't let him get away with it. I'll expose the real problems and then demonstrate drills to correct them.

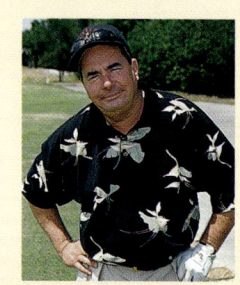

Watch out for Helpful Henry. He says things that sound like they should help your game, but they really may be keeping you from improving and playing better golf.

I believe that every golfer can play better! Improved play starts with a greater awareness of the direction in which the club is swinging and continues with knowing both what the clubface is doing during your swing and where you're hitting the ball on the clubface. It's also helpful to know that golf is a very hard game, and therefore progress will not always be swift.

It is very easy to misunderstand what people say. But you'll come away from this section with an enlightened understanding of how to substitute fact for fiction. Then you can begin practicing correctly to improve the quality of your game and increase your enjoyment of this wonderful sport.

IN THIS SECTION

Top Ten Misleading Terms and Analyses

- Keep the Left Arm Straight
- Keep the Clubhead Low to the Ground
- Turn, Turn, Turn
- Keep Your Head Down
- Swing Back Straight
- Extend, Extend, Extend
- Make a Weight Shift
- Swing Inside to Outside
- Swinging Over the Top
- Getting Trapped Behind

Why Aren't You Playing Better?

- Why the Clubface Position Is So Important
- Move Within the Move
- Swing Checkpoints
- Slice-Producing Problems
- Hook-Producing Problems

Instincts or Intellect: Which Is It?

- Meat-and-Potatoes Swing Changes
- Opposite Instincts
- Symmetrical Swing Plane
- No Concept/No Chance
- Not Staying with Corrections Long Enough
- Sweet Spot Search

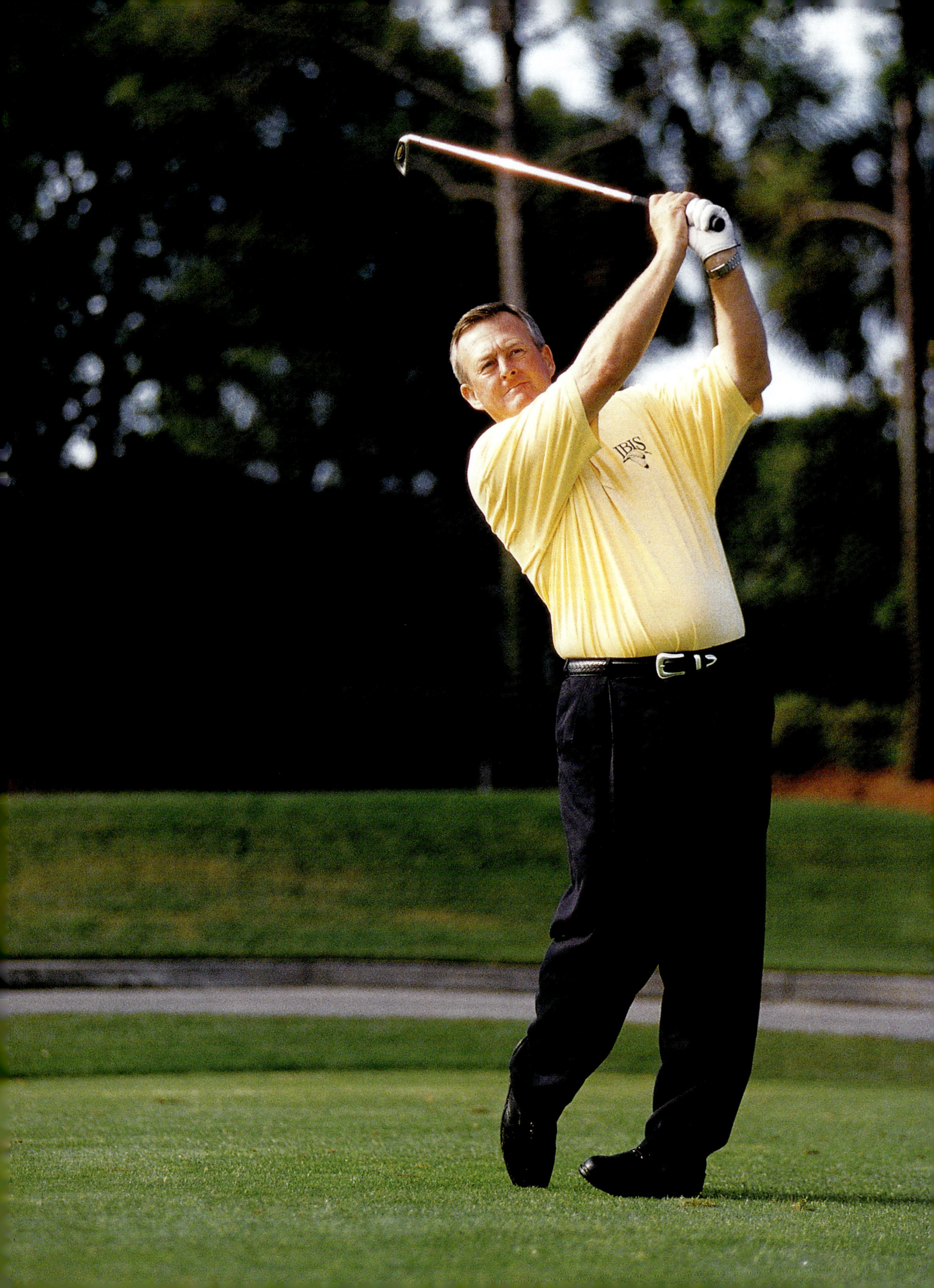
IBIS

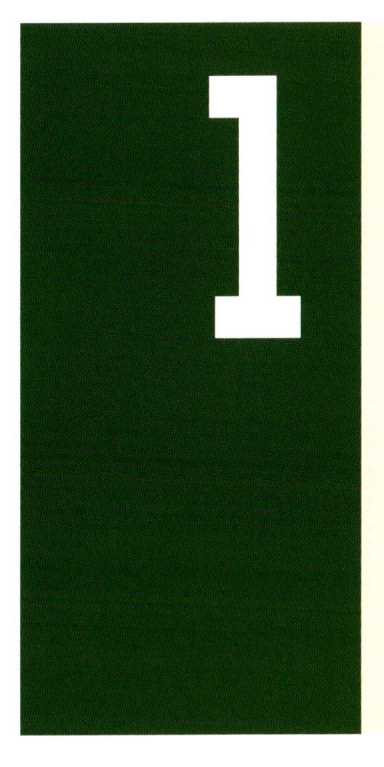

1 TOP TEN MISLEADING TERMS AND ANALYSES

Squaring the clubface to the target line at impact is what it's all about. If you're doing things in your swing that interfere with how the clubface should rotate correctly, you'll never play this game to your satisfaction!—Martin Hall

Myths and misconceptions come about because people sincerely want to help you. They're trying to encourage you, but they have no accurate idea of what to say. They probably don't have the experience or knowledge to actually tell you what you did wrong that caused the ball to dribble along the ground. It seemed perfectly logical to them that you must have lifted your head too early, which, as you'll soon find out, was probably not the cause at all.

Using this misinformation to correct the mistake usually leads to practicing the wrong things, making you even more frustrated when you can't correct the problem. It's like repeatedly dialing a wrong phone number. No matter how hard you try, you will never get through while using the wrong information. Albert Einstein's definition of insanity was, "Continuing to do what isn't working, then redoubling your efforts and yet expecting a different result." Unfortunately, that often applies to golfers in this situation.

To start playing better golf, eliminate the *Top Ten Misleading Terms and Analyses* that may be holding you back. I'll give you the correct information, along with some suggestions on how you can build a more skillful game.

Myth #1

Keep the Left Arm Straight

You didn't keep your left arm straight!

Every husband who ever watched his wife play may be equally as guilty as Henry if he told her she is bending her left arm during the swing. When the left arm bends or appears to bend, the real cause is the right arm overflexing. Following Helpful Henry's misleading advice results in a rigid left arm—freezing up the shoulder socket—that restricts the rotational motion and arm freedom needed in a good golf swing.

Searching for a reason for topping a golf ball, some golfers are either told or think they must have bent their left arm. Other golfers have the misconception that keeping the left arm straight creates a big wide swing arc. They believe the wider their arc, the farther their ball will go, which is only partly true.

Following Henry's bad advice is like starting a line of dominoes falling. As the following photos show, it makes your game worse, not better.

One Mistake Leads to Another

Martin demonstrates the problem caused by being obsessed with having a straight left arm.

Address

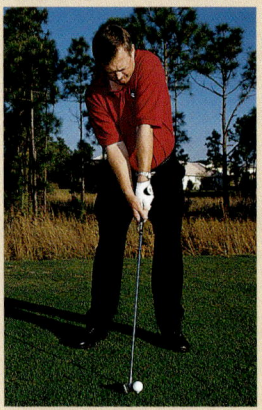

Notice how Martin follows Henry's bad advice by setting up with a rigid left arm. The shoulders have been forced into an incorrect tilt.

Backswing

The rigid left arm makes it very difficult, if not impossible, to get the club in the right slot as you finish the backswing. The detrimental effect is that the club is forced out of the proper swing plane.

Top of Backswing

Near the top of the backswing, the forced extension of the left arm locks up his shoulder sockets, preventing an unrestricted free-flowing rotation.

Past Impact

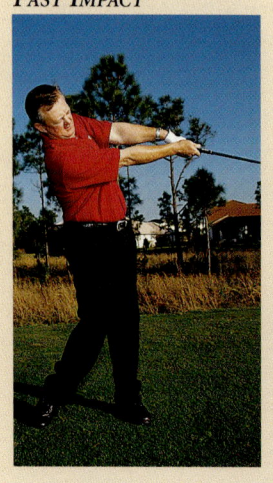

Forcing the left arm to be straight results in this virtually powerless position through impact. Locking up your arms steals power from your swing and reduces distance and accuracy from your shots.

Misconception

Forcing your left arm to be rigid can cause the following problems:

- Swaying off balance with the upper or lower body.
- Incorrect shoulder motion.
- Blocking of the clubface as it goes through the ball.
- Clubface open through the hitting area causes a slice.

THE TRUTH

You overflexed the right elbow.

You may think someone has bent their left arm, while in reality the problem was caused by overflexing the right elbow. Golf swings can be like a magician's sleight of hand—you think you've seen one thing while you've actually seen something quite different.

Here's how to see the truth. The next time you see a slow-motion version of a PGA TOUR player's swing, focus on the right elbow instead of the left arm.

It's what the *right arm* does that keeps the left arm straight! Your left arm can stay straight only because the right hand stays a certain distance from the left shoulder.

ENERGIZE YOUR CLUBHEAD

Energy can pass correctly through the arms to the clubhead—like water passes through a hose—if you do not lock up your shoulders. To keep the power flowing, try to keep your shoulders relaxed so your left arm does not stiffen during the backswing.

CORRECT ADDRESS

Notice the difference in Martin's shoulder tilt as he sets up to the ball without forcing his left arm to be rigid.

CORRECT BACKSWING

Martin prefers less than a 90-degree bend at the right elbow (dotted line). Your right arm should feel like it's pushing on the backswing.

CORRECT TOP OF BACKSWING

With his right elbow angle still under 90 degrees, Martin keeps his right hand the proper distance from his left shoulder, allowing him to remain on the correct swing plane.

PAST IMPACT

A free-flowing, powerful swing results when you don't force the left arm to be rigid, which locks up the shoulder joints.

MARTIN'S SWING THOUGHT

Instead of thinking about stretching your left arm, the right arm should always feel like it's pushing—pushing on the backswing and pushing on the follow-through.

Top Ten Misleading Terms and Analyses

17

CORRECTING THE PROBLEM

If you have the left-arm-straight syndrome firmly embedded in your mind, this drill will help you properly understand the role of the left arm during the swing. The left arm is too straight if:

1 - It looks like an iron rod hanging from the shoulder at setup.

2 - It *overextends* straight out during the backswing.

3 - It also *overextends* during the forward swing.

STRING DRILL

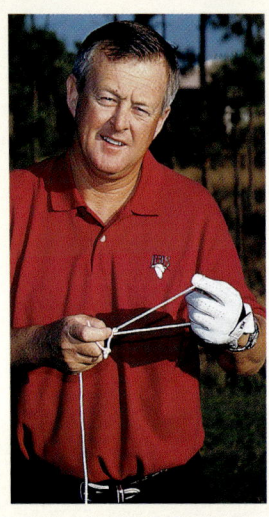

1-TIE THE STRING

2-LEFT HAND ON SHOULDER

3-BACKSWING

A piece of string keeps the right hand the proper distance from the body, correcting the bent left arm problem.

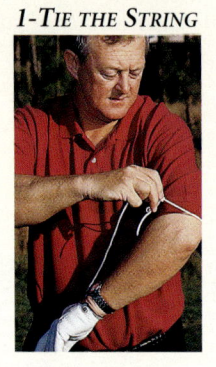

Using a slip knot, create a loop in a piece of string, then slip it onto your left arm above the elbow joint. Tighten the loop.

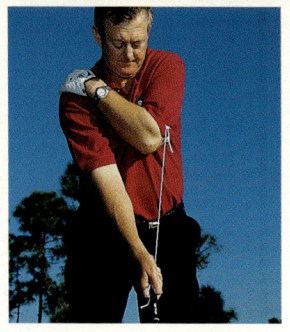

Put the loose end of the string on the club—as if it were a continuation of your left arm—and grip the club with your right hand. Place your left hand on your right shoulder.

What's keeping the string straight as Martin swings back? His right hand stays the same distance from the body as it was at setup. String is not able to stay straight by itself, proving that the control is linked to the right arm flex, which cures the bent left elbow problem.

This drill helps you understand that your left arm is not much more than a piece of string. To correct the real problem of a bending left arm, we need to correct the right arm from overflexing.

This drill will keep the right hand the correct distance from both the left shoulder and the body.

4-CORRECT RIGHT ARM FLEX

5-PROBLEM: OVERFLEXED

Notice how the string remains tight. Martin did not overflex his right arm, keeping the angle formed to less than 90 degrees.

See how the string is bent just as the left arm would be? The problem is the overflexed right elbow angle. Comparing this photo to the previous one (4) shows how exceeding 90 degrees causes your left arm to bend.

Establishing the correct right arm flex in your backswing is the cure, not trying to keep your left arm straight as Henry erroneously suggested!

MYTH #2

KEEP THE CLUBHEAD LOW TO THE GROUND

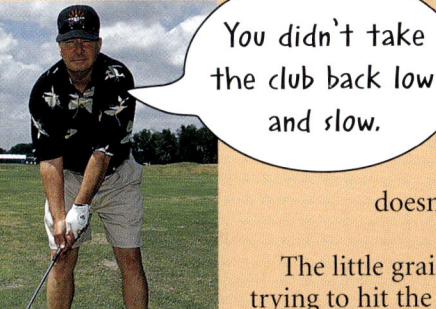

You didn't take the club back low and slow.

Henry's bad advice creates the idea that if you drag the clubhead back, brushing it along the ground for about a foot, that somehow you will hit the ball straighter. This contributes to the improper notion that maintaining this type of control over your backswing leads to accuracy. But it doesn't!

The little grain of logic that goes along with this idea is that since we are trying to hit the ball straight, let's try and keep the club straight to the ball.

But unlike pool, where you stand behind the ball with a cue, golfers stand to the side of the ball. Consequently, the club has to go up and down and inward.

BAD IDEA: KEEPING THE CLUBHEAD LOW TO THE GROUND

Dragging the clubhead back from the ball and along the ground will not help you hit accurate shots. The clubhead must follow a swing plane that goes up and around. The photos at right demonstrate the problem of taking the club back low. Slow can be okay as long as your overall swing has acceptable tempo.

Setup looks good.

Brushing the clubhead along the ground for about a foot of the takeaway is very bad advice. This prevents the clubhead from following the correct swing plane.

MISCONCEPTION

When television commentators speak in terms of taking a clubhead back low and slow, what they are really saying is: "The club is going smoothly up the plane." Trying to keep the clubhead low creates a balance problem, and then the arms start doing funny things.

Anytime you lose your balance, your arms make involuntary movements to recapture your balance. As a result, the entire golf swing resembles someone slipping on the ice or teetering on the edge of a swimming pool. If you lose your balance, you also lose any chance for hitting an accurate shot.

Keeping the clubhead low to the ground leads to these problems:

- Off-balance shots.
- You get too far behind the ball.
- You tend to hit the ground before striking the ball.
- Movement to correct your balance takes the club off the swing plane.
- The club must be redirected as it moves toward the ball.
- Clubhead speed is robbed.

The Truth

Swing back in a coordinated manner.

To hit the golf ball straight, you have the seemingly impossible task of getting two tiny little spots to meet—like the tips of two pencils. These spots are:

1 - The sweet spot of the club.

2 - The center of the ball.

The only way to hit accurate golf shots is to first understand that your golf swing is a tilted oval. Your clubhead lies on this imaginary swing plane that goes toward your target. Once a player understands that the swing plane is the total boss of the swing, a lot of these myths vanish.

The key is to maintain the radius of the swing to keep it on the correct plane. You don't want to extend or shorten it.

Maintain the Radius

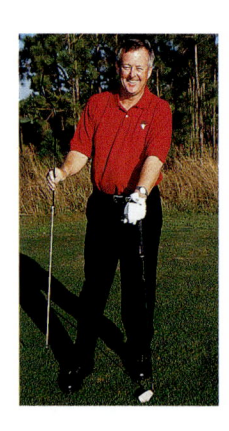

In vaudeville they used a hook to remove bad acts immediately from the stage. In this case I'm using a hook attached around my neck at one end and attached to my clubhead at the other end to demonstrate how the radius is maintained during a good golf swing. It's time to give the "hook" to Helpful Henry's bad advice.

Martin gives the hook to bad advice.

3-Maintain Swing Plane Radius

1-Set the Radius

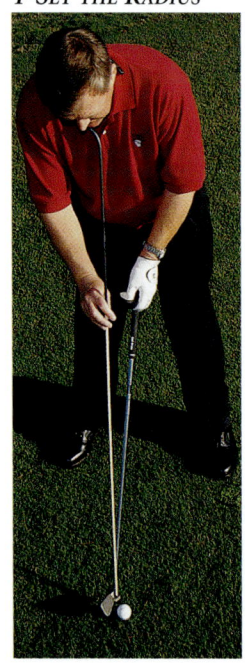

Demonstrating that the club does not go back low and straight but does go up and in, I'm putting this hook around my neck to set the center position of the swing. Attaching the pole with a magnet to my club sets the radius of the takeaway. See what happens given these two fixed constants.

2-Maintain Takeaway Radius

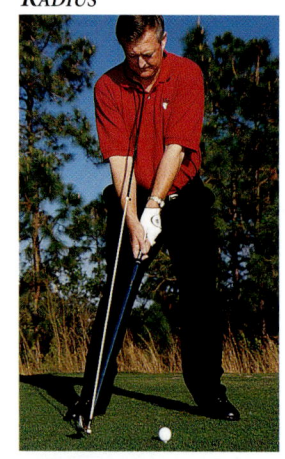

Takeaway begins with the hook around my neck and attached to the bottom of my club, ensuring the swing radius remains fixed at the same length.

The clubhead goes in and up, instead of straight back, as it follows the correct swing plane. Maintaining the radius established at setup allows me to stay on balance throughout my swing. My clubhead can stay on plane so the sweet spot of the clubhead can correctly meet the center of the ball at impact.

Golf Myths Exposed

Arc Drill

This is an excellent drill to help you start the clubhead back on the correct arc. You can also do this drill in your living room to develop the feel for the clubhead beginning its journey along the correct swing plane.

1-Set the Clubs

Place a club about one grip-length behind the ball. Set it at about 90 degrees to the target line. This is going to help you learn the proper takeaway arc.

2-Set your Address

Setting up properly to the ball at address, with the correct geometry, is vital to having the club's sweet spot impact the ball's center square to the target line.

3-Swing Back

Train yourself to begin following the correct swing arc. Swing the clubhead so that it arcs inward and upward, just missing the club on the ground. This approach is completely different from Henry's bad advice to take the club back low and slow.

4-Club Arcs

The clubhead should just pass over the grip when you use this drill to train your backswing to begin on the correct plane.

Top Ten Misleading Terms and Analyses

Myth #3

Turn, Turn, Turn

You're not turning enough.

Henry's statement has no real meaning in the golf world we all share. It's just a very misleading catchall phrase that in a nonexpert's mind covers what you must be doing wrong. So what's the harm? Plenty!

This innocent-sounding phrase leads to people turning so much that the club can't get on the proper swing plane. Have you noticed that the term "swing plane" keeps coming up as we talk about golf myths? By the way, what is it that you are supposed to keep turning anyway?

Over-turning

Hitting a golf shot requires turning, but the issue at hand is not to over-turn, which forces your clubhead off the correct swing plane. Should the Helpful Henrys of this world tell you to turn, turn, turn, here's what could happen.

Misconception

Golfers are always searching for power. Unfortunately, many believe that by really cranking, phenomenal, incredible power can be released to give the ball a big rip. Wrong!

Trying so hard to wind up negates any lateral motion in the swing. Humans can't turn around on a single axis point because we have a right *and* left hip joint. Instead we must turn on the right hip joint going back, and then shift to the left hip joint coming through.

- Over-turning does not allow the club to follow the correct swing plane.
- Your shots suffer from massive inconsistency. They can go all over the place, and do.

Address

Watch out for this position! This is where those last-minute detrimental swing thoughts can creep in (like "turn, turn, turn").

Backswing

Over-turning the trunk of my body at this position creates this around-the-body swing. The correct swing plane goes in and up, not around. The lower body has also over-turned at this point. A common mistake is to begin the takeaway with the hips and shoulders starting together. Your shoulders must turn more than your hips so they begin the swing linked to the arms, hands and club.

Reverse Pivot

Over-turning created this balance problem. I've turned so much that the weight incorrectly has ended up more toward my left leg.

Top of Backswing

This position reminds me of the old windup toys you may remember. What happened when you overwound them? They broke, just like this golf swing! A certain amount of turn is acceptable, but this is a classic over-turn situation caused by Helpful Henry's misleading advice.

Golf Myths Exposed

The Truth

Turn to follow the swing plane.

How much should you turn on your backswing? Just the right amount to let your club go up and down the swing plane. The only reason you turn your body is to make room for your hands and arms to go up and down this plane.

Knowing how much to turn also creates some torque, and this is easily accomplished by turning your upper body more than your lower body. Remember that backswings begin with the upper body while downswings begin with the lower body.

Turn to Keep the Club on Plane

AVOID THIS POSITION

Here, over-turning brought the club around my body. Instead of being on the correct plane, the butt is pointing to the right of the target.

Target Line

These photos show my club properly positioned on the swing plane. As the photos show, takeaway begins (1) with my shoulders, arms and hands. The lower body was pulled into the turn and its resistance to turning from the beginning creates torque.

At this vital checkpoint position (2), notice how the shaft of the club is correctly parallel to the target line. This guarantees the clubhead will be on the correct swing plane.

Martin Says

They will put this on my tombstone: "The purpose of the golf swing is to swing the club on a plane that has a relationship to the target."

Top Ten Misleading Terms and Analyses

Acceptable Body Turn

There is not really a formula for how much to turn, because the real key is to turn the right amount to let your club go up and down the swing plane. Below are the acceptable amounts of turn for your shoulders, hips and knees, so that you can create the torque needed to power your golf swing.

- 90 degrees of shoulder turn. Your back should be facing the target at the top of your backswing.

- 45 degrees for the hips. They need to turn only half as much as the shoulders.

- 22.5 degrees for the knees. They need to turn only half as much as the hips.

SWING PLANE DRILL

A large box from the supermarket will help teach you about your correct swing plane. There are two ways you can use it, and this drill is an excellent way to work on your swing plane at home.

1 You need to turn just so the shaft stays on the box in the lower part of your backswing and downswing. Done correctly, the box stays in position. Done incorrectly, the box is pushed away because you over-turned from the start of your backswing.

2 The second drill is to place the box about one-half inch away from the shaft. You should be able to swing up and down without the shaft hitting the box. Consult page 28 for additional information.

1-BACKSWING SWING PLANE

Set up with the shaft resting on the box (1). Begin your backswing with your shoulders, arms and hands, and the shaft will remain on the box without pushing it away on takeaway (2). The shaft is parallel to the target line, allowing the clubhead to go up and in following the swing plane (3). The club arrives at the top of my backswing with the butt of the grip pointing at the target line (4). Notice the amount of turn for my shoulders, hips and knees during these various views of my backswing, and compare that to the information on page 22.

2-DOWNSWING SWING PLANE

Following the swing plane brings the club's sweet spot and the ball's center together at impact. The hips began the downswing, and the shoulders, arms and hands are swinging the club powerfully down the plane. Notice the grip pointing to the target line (1). Just as it did on the backswing, the butt now points parallel to the target line in this key downswing checkpoint (2). Staying on plane, the shaft can again make contact with the box as the club enters the impact zone (3) and at impact (4). Following the swing plane is the only way to hit consistent golf shots: The club arrives at the ball square-to-the-target-line.

Myth #4

Keep Your Head Down

You looked up too early.

The derivation of this really old myth may be attributable to some old Scottish pro, because it has plagued us for a couple of centuries. The expression should really be, "I have no idea what you did, so I'll tell you that you lifted your head up." My suggested answer whenever you hear this worthless advice is, "So you really don't know what I did!"

Making an unnatural effort to keep the head down tightens the neck muscles, which tightens the shoulders, and then you end up with no body pivot or speed at all—and that is a major problem. The correct swing tip should be: Maintain a steady head.

The Problem: The Unsteady Head

Good golf swings feature a steady head, but that's different from Henry's bad advice about looking up early. In essence, he's telling you to force your head down. Let's look at the swing problems this causes.

Mistake: Head Down

Mistake: Shoulders Hit Chin

Good Head Position at Address

Keeping your head down tightens the muscles of the neck, ultimately restricting the all-important body pivot.

Keeping your chin down at address leads to the shoulders bumping into it during the backswing.

The chin should be out at address to prevent the neck from locking. This also allows your shoulders to rotate under the chin on your backswing.

Misconception

The confusion with Henry's advice is that golfers often misunderstand the difference between keeping the head down and keeping it steady. To make golf swings work, you must turn the body one way and then turn it the other way. Your arms have to go up and down the plane and, at the same time, your head does have to stay fairly steady. Today's technology allows the swings of the best players to be critically analyzed, and it proves their heads move very little.

THE TRUTH

Maintain a steady head during your swing.

Earlier in my teaching career I worked for Jack Nicklaus. I learned how his instructor, Jack Grout, would literally hold Jack's hair to keep his head steady during a swing. I've done several clinics with Tom Watson, and he said the best thing he ever did was practice with his shadow in front of him to see if his head was moving. Watson always sought out a spot on a practice range that offered this potential to improve. Unfortunately, many people shy away from having their shadow in front of them because they believe it inhibits their concentration. Actually, having the sun cast your shadow in front of you can be very instructive.

MARTIN SAYS

A good mental image would be to see your head and shoulders sticking out of a hotel window in New Orleans, where they have really small windows. See yourself swinging back and forth held in place by the window frame.

STILL-HEAD DRILL

1-SETUP

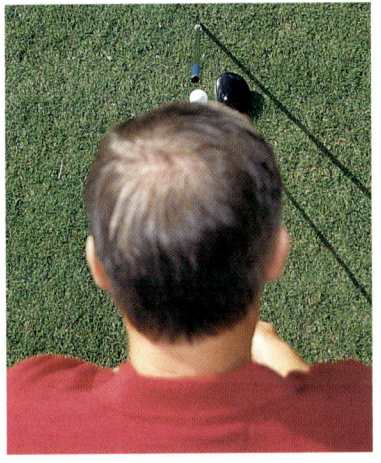

Place a shaft opposite the ball so it points to your head. The key to this drill is that you feel as if you are looking right down the shaft all the way through your swing as if it were a gun barrel. You should never see the side of the shaft.

2-STILL HEAD ON BACKSWING

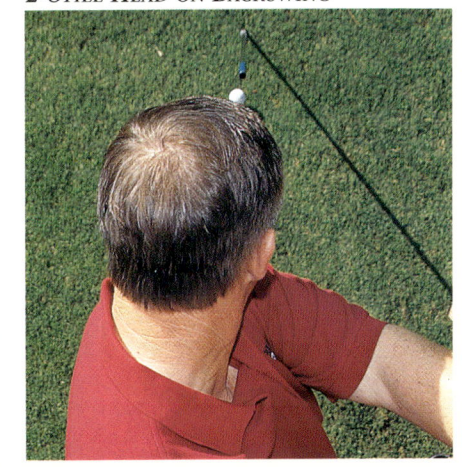

As the club reaches the top of your backswing, the shaft should still be pointing to your head.

3-STEADY HEAD IMPACT

Through impact, the shaft is still pointing to your head. Keeping your forward bend constant also gives the appearance that your head remained steady.

4-FOLLOW-THROUGH/NATURAL ROTATION

The rotation of your shoulders brings the head up. Following Henry's misinformed advice will limit the amount of body pivot, resulting in a loss of speed. Remember to keep your head steady, *not* down.

Top Ten Misleading Terms and Analyses

MYTH #5

SWING BACK STRAIGHT

You didn't take the club back straight.

In this case poor old Henry can't take all the blame. Some of it must be shared by those television commentators who will tell you that "Tiger Woods hits it so straight because he goes down the line longer than anybody else." That's absolutely not true at all! The only thing you want to go down the target line is the ball.

It's tempting, I admit, to think that if you swing back and forth straight, you will make the ball go straight. But here's the problem. There are no straight lines anywhere in a golf swing because it's really a tilted circle, and circles have no straight lines. It all gets back to the swing plane.

DON'T BE FOOLED

Trying to swing back straight is an easy trap to fall into because it seems like such a logical way to hit straight shots. But it's detrimental because it results in severe loss of power. Croquet and pool are sports where the stroke is straight back and forth. This is golf, and if you try to swing back straight, the photos show how to detect it.

I'm using a large cardboard box as a detection aid to place the toe of the club against. You can also use a wall.

ADDRESS

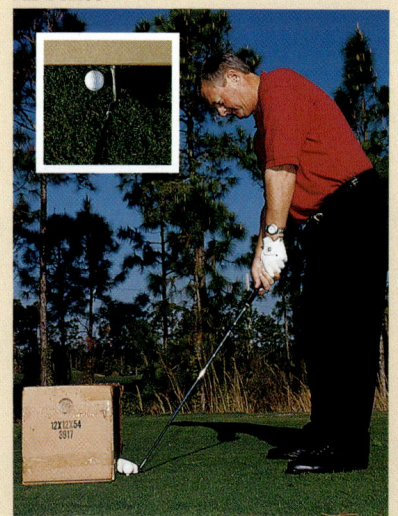

To detect if you are swinging straight back, begin by placing the toe of the club against a box or a wall.

INCORRECT TAKEAWAY

As you swing back, if the toe of the club remains in contact with the box or wall, you have fallen for some very bad advice. The club is incorrectly following a straight line instead of the tilted swing plane circle.

INCORRECT BACKSWING CONTINUATION

During this stage the straight backswing begins to send the clubhead almost vertically up in the air, and that's why it is still incorrectly touching the box. Golf is not a vertical game, because we must stand on the side of the ball. Swing planes are tilted circles.

MISCONCEPTION

Some people take the club back straight because they are trying to avoid doing something incorrectly. They are trying to keep the club from going in the wrong direction on the backswing. If you are incorrectly attempting to swing along a straight line, you already must have noticed these problems:

- You cannot pivot correctly to make a proper turn.
- You hit a lot of slices.
- You hit a lot of topped or fat shots because you're unable to get a good angle of attack.

THE TRUTH

Swing on an arc.

Don't make the mistake of trying to control the part of the swing you have the least control over! Where the clubhead meets the ball (impact) is where the club is going its fastest and is where we have the least control over it.

You must trust the correct swing plane, and that plane is a tilted circle, not a straight line. Croquet is a vertical game, but golf certainly is not. Golfers stand to the side of the ball, the shaft goes into the clubhead at an angle, and that angle dictates where the club must swing. You can't swing back and through the ball along a straight line and still play decently.

TILTED CIRCLE DRILL

As I use a swing plane training aid along with the box, compare these photos with the incorrect straight-back photos (page 28) to see how the clubhead must follow the swing plane's tilted circle.

1-CORRECT SETUP

2-CORRECT TAKEAWAY

3-CORRECT BACKSWING CONTINUATION

Once again I'm using the box as a reference point for the toe of my club, but this time the shaft is resting on a swing plane training aid. The circle shows the angle at which the shaft enters the clubhead, and this angle dictates where the swing must go.

I swing back with the shaft resting on the swing plane aid. Notice how the club's toe is already swinging back inside of the box instead of staying on it.

Following the tilted swing plane, the club is on a much different track than in the incorrect photos (page 28). The toe is away from the box. Following the swing plane is the only way to build and release the power needed for distance-producing, accurate shots. Swing along the circle instead of straight back.

I have some outstanding swing plane drills for you in Chapter 4.

Top Ten Misleading Terms and Analyses

Myth #6

Extension

Extend way back for more power.

Our tipster Henry would have you believe that the more extended you are going back and through, the farther you will hit the ball. A lot of myths are linked to the eternal quest for golf's Holy Grail: more distance.

Archimedes said, "Give me a lever long enough and a place to stand, and I can move the earth." Hitting a golf ball, however, does not require the leverage of an overextended shaft. Clubhead speed is really created by both the rotary motion of the hips and shoulders going through the ball, and by the lever action. This creates far greater speed than trying to extend to an artificial width during the swing.

Incorrect Attempt to Artificially Widen the Arc

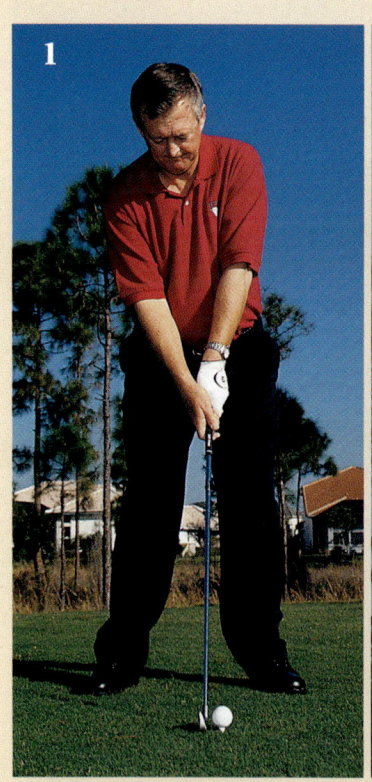

Even advanced players can fall prey to this erroneous tip. They begin with an excellent setup (1) and then stretch their arms out of their shoulder sockets (2) going back. The key to proper extension is to maintain what you had in the setup position.

Misconception

Looking at the still photos of excellent players' swings, like Seve Ballesteros in his prime or Davis Love, we can't help marveling at their wide extension. But you really need to see them without a club to determine how long their arms naturally are. Their extension, the one you may want to emulate, was predetermined by their parents. It's purely genetic. If their arms are 36 inches long, that's why they have a very wide swing arc. We are all subject to genetics; consequently, the length of our arms will determine the proper width of our swing arcs.

The Truth

Maintain what you created at your setup.

Instead of thinking in terms of *extension*, substitute a more helpful word for the correct swing arc: *maintenance*. Maintaining the distance between the nape of your neck to the grip end of the club is the key for the proper width of your swing arc.

It's like a spoke in a wheel. The spoke doesn't get longer as the wheel is turning, yet that's what Henry's misleading advice would have you believe. Maintaining the radius of the golf swing is what you really need to do for permanent improvement.

Spokes in a Wheel

Just like spokes in a wheel, your hands move around a steady center.

It's certainly a misconception to believe that with a wider arc you can swing faster. What you end up with is a buckled wheel that bulges out in certain spots.

Widening your arc will surely destroy your smooth swing. The action photo of the swing and wheel at right provides the correct mental image of the natural width of your swing plane.

The distance between Martin's neck and the grip end of his club is maintained all the way through his swing, just like the spokes of a wheel.

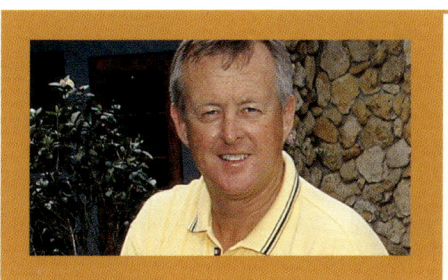

Martin Says

You can have a wider swing arc, but unless you hit the ball in the center of the clubface, it doesn't matter. One-quarter inch off the sweet spot and you give up 10 to 15 percent of your distance. One-half inch off the sweet spot costs you a 30 to 40 percent loss of distance.

Top Ten Misleading Terms and Analyses

Natural Swing Arc Drill

This drill helps cure the overextension syndrome while at the same time it fortifies in your mind how to maintain what you created at the setup position.

1-Set the Width of the Arc

To place the bag the correct distance away for the drill, start with the ball in the correct position in your stance. Extend the club outward from the outside of your right foot to provide a point to place your bag.

2-Setup

Take your normal setup position.

3-Good: Correct Extension

As you swing back, the club should not hit your golf bag.

4-Bad: Forced Extension

If the club hits your bag on the backswing, you are forcing the extension. Photo 3 shows my arms in good position. In the good position, I maintain my setup distance. Photo 4 shows my arms in bad position. In the bad position, you can see I'm obviously following Henry's poor advice and trying to artificially extend my swing arc, which doesn't create distance and accuracy.

Myth #7

Weight Shift

Shift all the way to the right and then all the way to the left.

Henry's misleading weight-shift tip is the equivalent of getting a tip from a friend to buy a certain stock at $2 because it's a *sure thing* to reach $50 a share. Some people get so obsessed with thinking about more weight shift, instead of pivoting to the right and left, that they get pulled off center and fail to deliver a real *punch* to the ball at impact.

Instead of that long-flying, laser-accurate shot they hoped to hit, they end up with inconsistent efforts that sadly lack *both* length and accuracy. You do need to shift some weight during your swing, but the key is to pivot and coil, not overshift.

The Problem

Putting some rope around a shaft angled in the ground and using a second shaft for a reference point, I'll demonstrate how you get pulled off center by following Henry's shifting advice.

Misconception

Most talk about shifting weight has to do with correcting a reverse pivot, where the weight is over the wrong foot at the wrong time in the swing. Henry's misinformation—while partially correct in maintaining that you do have to transfer some weight—leads to the problem that I demonstrated.

Incorrectly shifting the weight and swaying is responsible for these problems:

- Hitting the ball off the toe of the club.
- Hitting thin shots.
- Difficulty in finding the ball on the downswing.

SETUP

SWAYING BACK AND FORTH

You can check your weight shifting by:

- Placing a rope around a shaft angled in the ground and gripping both ends.
- Placing another shaft in the center as a reference point.

Trying to increase weight shift can lead to swaying back and forth instead of pivoting. Notice how the right knee wobbles and sways, making it hard to get to the ball on the way down.

Top Ten Misleading Terms and Analyses

33

The Truth

Coil-shift-uncoil.

The key here is to think less about weight shift and more about the correct pivot. Golf is a "windup and then an unwind" game! To improve your game you must unwind as you move through the shot. Here's a simple order of weight-transfer motion to remember:

1 - Backswing: Shift to the right and coil.

2 - Downswing: Shift to the left and uncoil.

3 - Think of impact as the *big punch*.

The Big Punch Drill

1-Backswing Pivot

2-Downswing Pivot

Martin Says

What's truly misleading is the belief that any one tip can make any substantial difference to what is a complex motor skill. When a player has a good concept of the motion of the swing, then all of these bad tips melt away.

Properly pivoting is the real "punch" in golf. It's just like a boxer punching that ball and scoring a knockout blow. This is the correction for Henry's misleading tip and an outstanding drill to practice at home. Using the same rope drill setup, this is how a correct weight shift and pivot should look and feel.

Pulling back with your right hand provides the feeling you need to make the correct backswing pivot. I would like to see 65 percent of your weight on the right foot and 35 percent of your weight on the left foot.

Pulling back with the left hand provides the feeling you need to make the correct downswing pivot that delivers a mighty punch to the ball.

MYTH #8

SWING INSIDE TO OUTSIDE

To stop slicing or fading, swing inside to outside.

Henry has given us a tricky tip here. I once fell victim to this earlier in my career, and it took a while to shake it. It's tricky, because for someone who incorrectly swings from outside the target line to inside the target line, trying to swing from in to out is actually a very good feel.

But, and there is a very big but to this, if that person ever really starts swinging inside the target line to outside the target line, here's what will happen:

1 - Pushed shots to the right.

2 - Hooks.

3 - Thin hits.

4 - Abysmal short game.

INCORRECT INSIDE-TO-OUTSIDE SWING

I've placed some wooden sticks on the ground to represent my target line, and I've teed the ball up in the center of the sticks. This method is excellent for determining your present swing path.

MISTAKE: INSIDE RETURN TO THE BALL

The clubhead is returning to the ball from a severe inside approach. The clubhead should correctly follow an inside-to-square-to-inside swing path, but this swing won't be able to because I'm demonstrating swinging to the right, which takes the clubhead past the line after impact.

MISTAKE: INCORRECT IMPACT ZONE POSITION

Entering the impact zone, the clubhead is approaching the ball too much from the inside of the target line. This approach will not allow the clubhead to become square to the target line at impact, and an off-target shot will result. Remember, a ball does what it is told to do.

MISTAKE: PAST THE LINE

Henry's inside-to-outside swing tip has now incorrectly brought the clubhead outside the target line when it should be returning to an inside-the-line path after impact. The clubhead position clearly shows it was not square to the line at impact.

MISCONCEPTION

The best way to make friends for life with a slicer is to give him or her the magical solution that will forever end their big banana shot path from left to right. One reason for slicing is a swing path that comes from outside the target line to inside the line with the face of the club open at impact, slicing across the ball.

The misconception is that slicers simply need to change their swing path to *in to out*, and they will draw the ball, getting extra distance as a bonus. As I said earlier it might indeed be a good feeling to help correct a slicer's problem with this advice, but it is far from the cure and leads down the wrong path.

The Truth

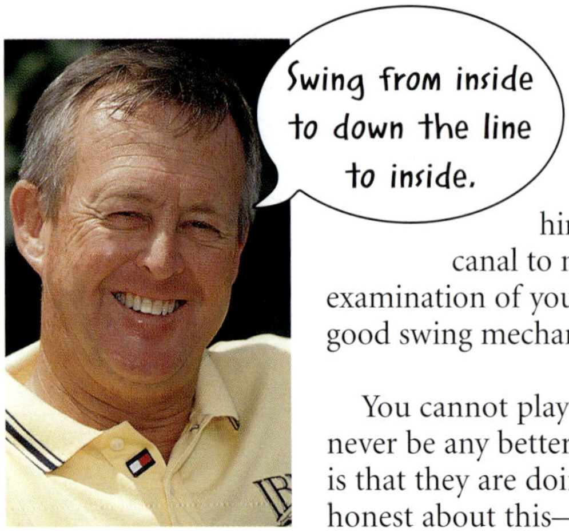

Swing from inside to down the line to inside.

I doubt you would want to go into a dentist's office, have him quickly open your mouth and say, "Yup, looks like a root canal to me!" You would first want an X ray and a thorough examination of your mouth. Correct diagnosis is more than half the cure, and good swing mechanics are the only medicine to heal a troubled swing.

You cannot play golf consistently without good mechanics, because you will never be any better than your fundamentals. One assumption many players make is that they are doing just one thing wrong when in reality—and I'm just being honest about this—most of what they do may not be very good at all.

Such is the case with Henry's misleading advice in this situation about substituting one bad swing plane for another. It's just not correct and you won't improve by falling for it.

The Only Swing Plane

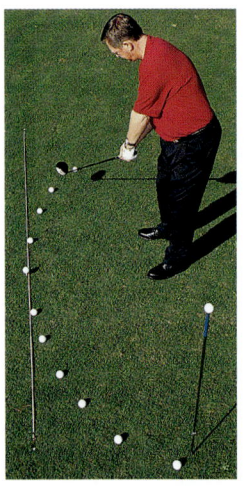

The golf balls on the ground illustrate the only long-game swing plane that will improve your length and accuracy.

IMPACT

PAST IMPACT

The club's sweet spot must strike the center of the ball and be square to the target line at the point of impact! That's the goal, and because we stand to the side of the ball, the club must follow a tilted circle created by:

1. A backswing that follows a path from square to inside.

2. A downswing that goes from inside, returns to square at impact, and then returns to an inside path.

The clubhead returns to a square-to-the-target-line position at impact, after approaching the ball along the arc shown. This is a circle, and circles do not have straight lines or bulges that are caused by many of the misinformed swing tips you receive. The ball on the shaft is used in a drill to help you develop the correct path after impact.

Tracing the circle, the clubhead returns to inside the target line after impact. At no time did the clubhead ever pass over the target line. Once you set up to the target, the only thing you want going down the line is the ball.

RETURN TO THE INSIDE DRILL

To get immediate feedback about your swing, place a ball on a tall shaft inside the target line and along the correct swing arc. Then hit the ball off the tee as you follow through. Practice this drill slowly to develop the feeling for this correct long-game swing plane.

Myth #9

You're Swinging Over the Top

Should someone give you this advice, immediately ask them this question: "What am I swinging over the top of? Am I over the top of the target line? The swing plane? What exactly do you mean?" The silence of their response will be deafening.

You came over the top.

Generally, when someone gives you this tip, they mean you are swinging from outside the target line to inside the target line. That's the same as swinging a little left of your target, and when this occurs it's a by-product of hitting too many slices. You're compensating for the direction the ball is presently going in.

Here are some of the problems this swing brings:

1 - Lots of pulled balls to the left.

2 - Low fades.

3 - Topping the ball occasionally.

4 - Cavernous divots caused by the very steep angle of attack.

5 - An okay short game, but horrible drives.

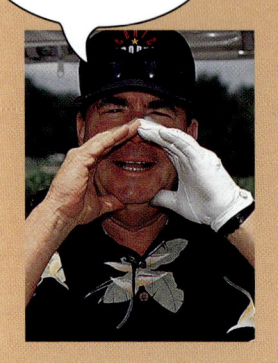

Incorrect Outside-to-Inside Swing Plane

Does your clubhead approach the ball from outside the target line? Here's a simple way for you to analyze your own golf swing—without relying on the Helpful Henrys of this world—and correctly diagnose the problem right now.

Spear the Noodle

I've cut a chunk out of a child's foam rubber swimming pool noodle, which you can find wherever pool toys are sold. I inserted an old shaft halfway into it so it's flexible at its end. I positioned it a foot behind the ball at an inclined angle that allows the clubhead to pass underneath it if the swing path is correct. An outside-to-inside swing plane will be easy to detect, because the shaft will hit the noodle.

Make Some Swings

The shaft hits the noodle and provides immediate feedback if the swing path to the ball follows an outside-to-inside path.

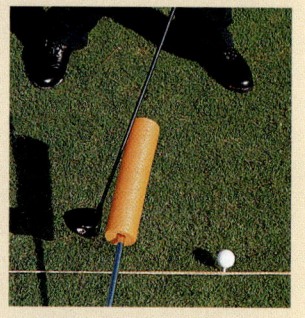

Outside-to-inside swing paths approach the ball on a very steep angle of attack, as seen in this photo.

Misconception

An outside-to-inside swing plane does not cause slices. Rather, it is a symptom of slicing. Only one thing causes a slice, and that is an open clubface.

Why would a player have this swing plane? It's not something done on purpose. This is the manifestation of golf's survival mechanism, an involuntary movement. Hit enough slices to the right, and soon you'll be swinging to the left to stop it from flying to the right. If I gave you a car that kept steering to the right, it wouldn't take you very long to steer to the left to keep the car on the road.

Golf Myths Exposed

THE TRUTH

Stay on plane.

Could you aim a rifle if every time you fired it the bullets went in a different direction? The same thing is true when aiming a golf club. If your swing can't repeat itself, you will be unable to aim.

You can change everything if you change what the face of the club is doing. If you can't do this, then you change just about nothing. Just as with our last myth, the only way to play better golf is to develop the correct inside-to-square-to-inside swing arc. The club should never cross the target line either prior to impact or after impact.

UNDER-THE-NOODLE DRILL

Another cause of the outside-to-inside swing plane comes from trying to muscle the ball. The old distance devil bites again: Trying to muscle the ball turns the shoulders to get your weight shifting into the shot early. Unless golfers are very well trained, they will over-accelerate their hands and arms from the top.

Using the noodle setup, practice swinging the club along the correct swing plane, bringing it under the noodle.

1-Downswing Checkpoint

I've laid a club on the ground parallel to the target line. On the downswing, it should look to you like the club in your hands covers the one on the ground. The butt of your club should be pointed parallel to the target line on the backswing and here on the downswing.

2-Correct Approach

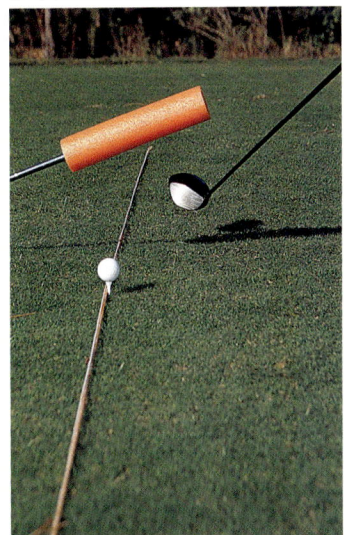

Once you correctly reach the checkpoint of the shaft being parallel to the target line, it's very easy to swing the clubhead under the noodle as you follow the correct swing arc.

Myth #10

Trapped Behind

Just like Tiger, you got trapped.

Henry is passing along a tip he heard Tiger Woods say. It seems every time Tiger doesn't play very well he tells the press in the media room exactly what Henry said above: "I got trapped behind and I'm flipping it."

Translation: Tiger means he is swinging too much to the right, too much from in to out. I can only say to the rest of the golfing world, "I only hope you get trapped behind like Tiger does. You wish!"

This could also be considered the current *Tip of the Tiger* era just as there was a tip of the Palmer, Nicklaus and Watson eras when they were the leading players and it became fashionable to suffer from the same golfing malaise they did. But back then, the same as now, whatever the problem, it probably was not the reason that golfers sliced or duffed their shots.

The Real Trap

What is Tiger trapped behind? He's trapped behind the plane and will end up swinging to the right of the target. It's a mistake made by good players. Using my target line and another line placed parallel to it at waist high, I'll demonstrate what getting trapped really looks like.

TRAPPED POSITION

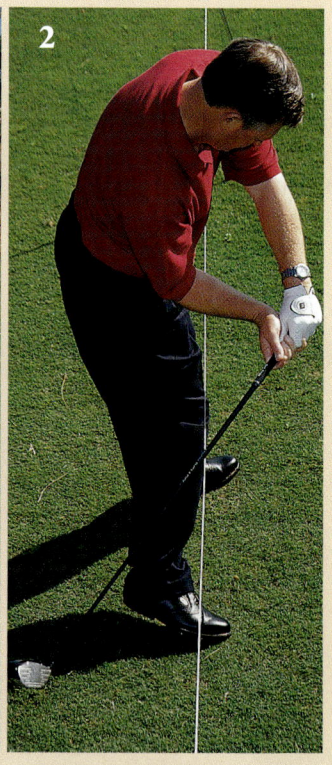

In both of these views you can see the club is not in the correct swing plane that golfers need for consistently long and accurate shots. In photo 1, the club looks like it's out of sync with the downswing pivot. The view from above (2) shows that the grip of the club is not in front of my chest, forming a triangle with my arms and chest, but rather is outside the target line when it should be parallel to the line. To reach impact requires flipping the wrists and arms, an action that closes the clubface too quickly.

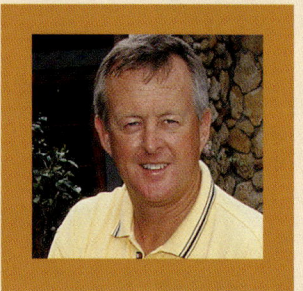

Martin Says

In this book we will abandon confusing golf terminology, and instead think and talk in simple, understandable terms such as *right* or *left* (rather than *inside* or *outside*), *over the top* and *underneath*.

Misconception

Golf terminology can lead to the confusion and misunderstanding. For example, why is it that when the clubface is pointed to the right we say the clubface is *open* but when the shoulders are pointed to the right we say they are *closed?* Swing your club to the right and it's referred to as *in to out.*

Wouldn't it be easier if we just said this is going to the right and this to the left? Some terminology leads to the confusion because it doesn't make any sense at all.

The Truth

> Your club shaft must be parallel to the target line on the downswing.

The club can really only be swung in one of three directions: to the target; to the right of the target; to the left of the target.

Good golf employs basic geometry, and I believe and teach that whenever you are trying to hit a straight shot, the shaft should be parallel to the target line on both the backswing and downswing, when it is also parallel to the ground.

What makes me so certain of this? Club and ball manufacturers build super-sophisticated machines to test their products, and the key is that they must have the machines hit straight shots. With all the research dollars and testing at their beck and call, their robots have the shaft parallel to the target line during the backswing and downswing when it is also parallel to the ground. Can you think of anything more repeatable than *Iron Byron's* swing?

Parallel-to-the-Target-Line Drill

Notice the difference in the two photos seen here when compared to the trapped swing photos on page 40.

1 - Takeaway

2 - Downswing

In the trapped swing the club has to swing to the right. Once I reach the parallel-to-the-target-line position, it's easy to just swing down and through the ball. Visualizing I'm standing behind a barbed wire fence (1), the correct takeaway position keeps my clubhead in front of the fence keeping it from getting stuck in the wire. On the downswing (2) as my club reaches the power slot position, with the shaft parallel to the target line in front of the fence, I can now swing down and through without getting the clubhead trapped in the wire.

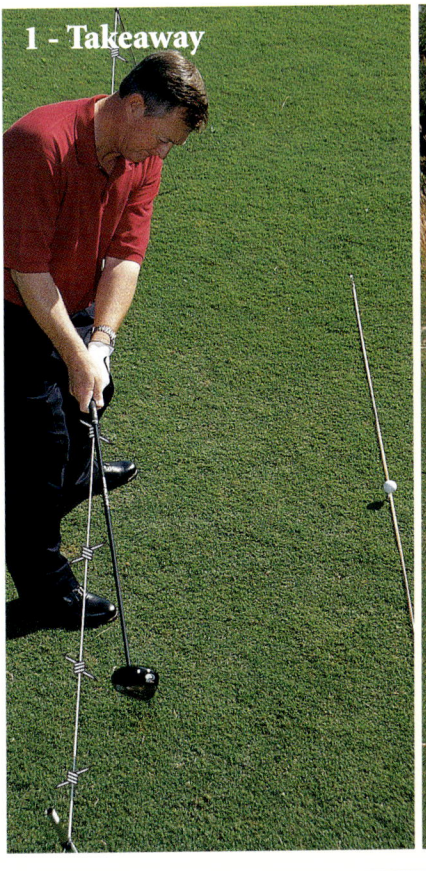

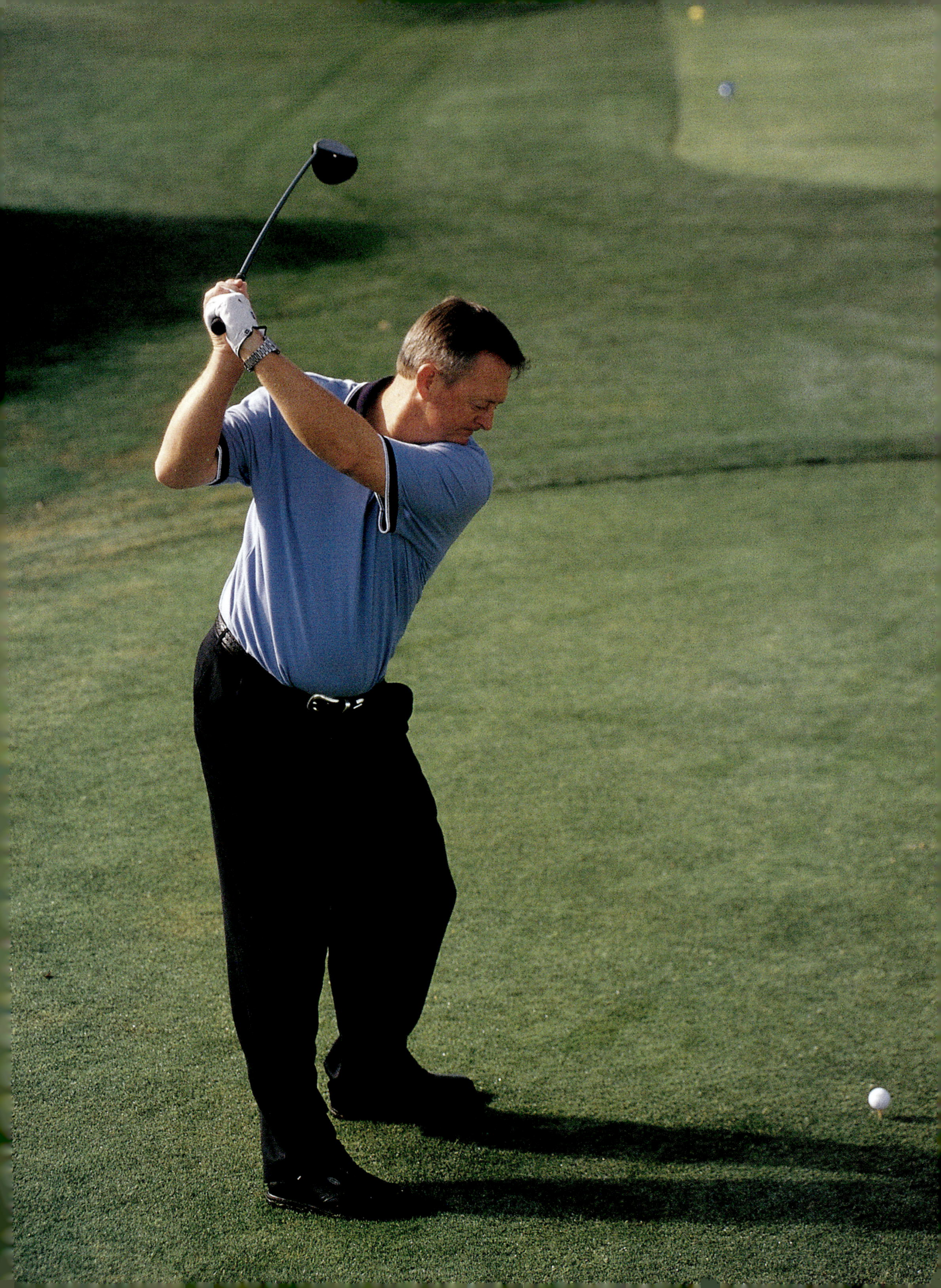

2 WHY AREN'T YOU PLAYING BETTER?

The reason most golfers do not play better is that they do not understand the enormous effect the clubface can have in shaping and influencing their golf swing.
—Martin Hall

So why aren't you playing better golf? Balls don't go into the water or out of bounds because they have it in for you. Do you really believe golf gods exist? If not, then who are you berating as you look to the sky, with your arms flailing in the air, venting your frustration for hitting a poorly executed shot?

Or maybe you're one of those individuals who blames the devil while you stomp your foot or bash a club into the ground. The real problem boils down to the essence of the golf swing. **What did your clubface do during the swing? Did it rotate correctly?**

270 Degrees of Rotation

If golf were like croquet or cricket (the sport of my youth), it would be really easy to master, because they don't require any clubface rotation to hit the ball. But golfers must rotate the clubhead 270 degrees during the swing. The one and only time the clubface must be square to the target line is when the ball leaves it, and that's the *No. 1* goal to strive for.

Golfers fail to improve because few really understand the vitally important role of clubhead rotation. Practice sessions are devoted only to curing the symptoms, not the problem. That's a normal reaction, because understanding clubhead rotation is not something you just stumble upon. Some people develop this intuitively without even knowing they are doing it, while others, to their grave misfortune, are duped by misconceptions, resulting in either a restricted clubface rotation or overrotating it too early in the swing.

Great players have the clubface square to the target line once and only once—*when the ball leaves the clubface.* Many good players do not have the clubface set up square at address! Believing the clubface must be set up square at address is a misconception. So if your clubhead is facing right (the open position) when the ball leaves it or facing left (the closed position) just one or more degrees, the ball will deviate away from your target line by the amount of yards listed in the chart below.

Golf's real challenge is squaring the clubface as you launch the ball. There are obviously several things that influence the clubface. There is the *big move,* which everybody can see when the shoulders are curled first in one direction and the arms and club go up the plane, creating a nice-looking swing.

> **MARTIN'S BASIC RULE**
>
> The ball can only go where the clubface sends it.
>
> - If the ball goes to the right, the face was pointed to the right when the clubface impacted the ball.
> - If the ball goes to the left, the face was pointed to the left when the clubface impacted the ball.

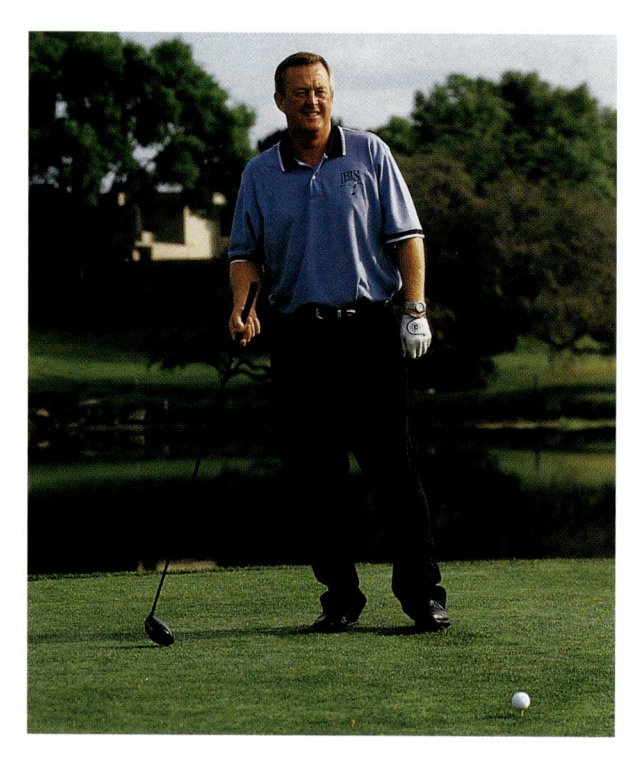

You can have a beautiful swing with a wonderful plane, but unless the clubface is square to the target line at impact, the results will not be acceptable. Camouflaged in there is a *move within the move: the turning of the clubface.*

Degrees Off Line at Impact	Shot Distance	Off Line
1 degree	200 yards	12 yards
2 degrees	200 yards	24 yards
3 degrees	200 yards	36 yards
4 degrees	200 yards	You won't find it!

MOVE WITHIN THE MOVE

The 270 degrees of clubhead rotation during the golf swing (90 degrees on the backswing plus 180 degrees on the downswing for a total of 270 degrees) is the *move within the move*. Using a badminton racket, club and clock face makes it easier to see and understand.

Martin demonstrates the all-important move within the move.

90-DEGREE BACKSWING ROTATION

SETUP

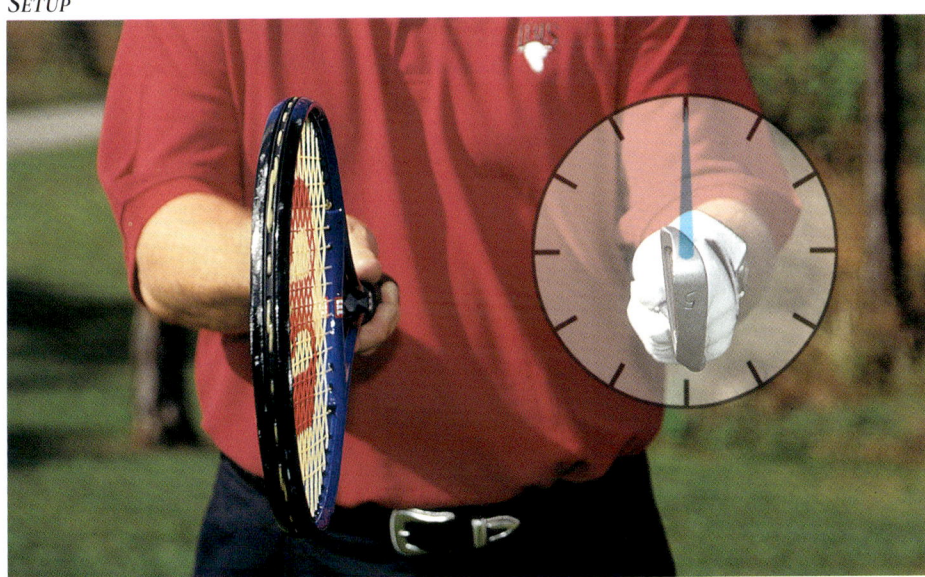

The clubface should be vertical at setup, just like the racket. Using a clock to provide a reference point, the 12 o'clock position should be square to the target line. The rest of the photos give two different clock positions as a reference. The first presents the correct time from the photo view and the second gives you the time reference when you swing the club.

TOP OF BACKSWING

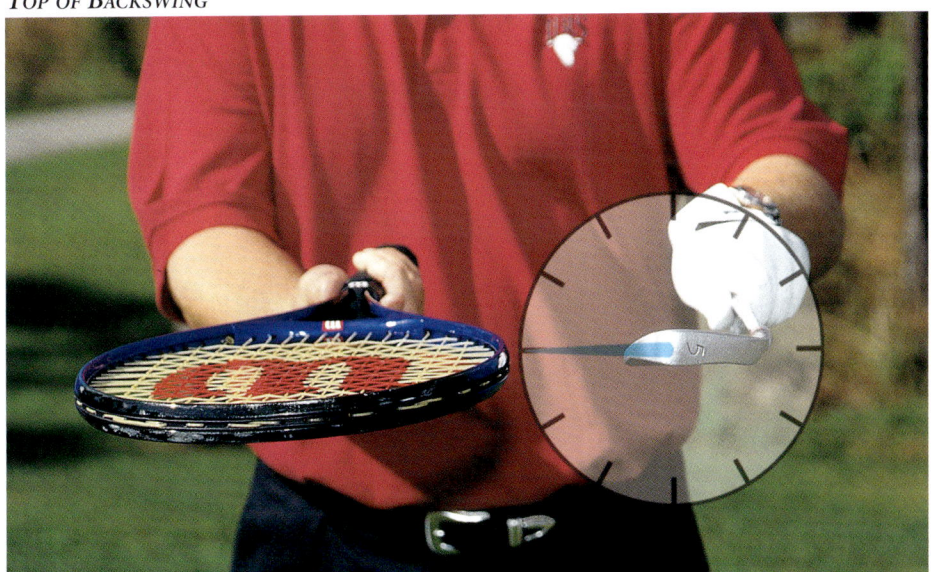

The arms, wrists and hands rotate the clubface 90 degrees during the backswing.

- The clubface points to the 9 o'clock position from this view.

- As you would look at it while swinging back, the clubface rotation will point the top edge to 3 o'clock.

180-Degree Downswing Rotation

From the backswing position, the arms and hands must rotate the clubface 90 degrees back to the 12 o'clock square position and then another 90 degrees going through.

COMMON SENSE TERMINOLOGY

As a teacher who must help his students understand and master the complexities of golf, I question if the game's terminology is not even more complicated than the game itself. As an example:

1. If a clubhead points left of the target line at address, it's referred to as closed. But if the feet point to the left at address, they're considered to be in an open position.

2. If a clubhead points right of the target line at address, it's referred to as open. But if the feet point to the right at address, they're considered to be in a closed position.

I believe some misleading terminology leads to misconceptions that take golfers down the incorrect roads. For clarity this book refers to *left* and *right* positions.

TRANSITION

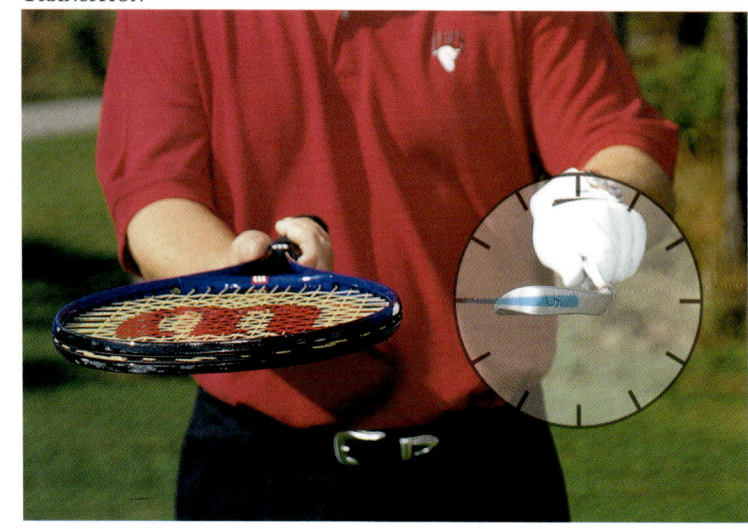

The downswing begins from the following clock positions based on your view.

- *9 o'clock position when seen from this angle.*
- *3 o'clock from your view as you swing.*

90-DEGREE IMPACT

The arms, wrists and hands rotate the clubface 90 degrees counterclockwise in the opposite direction to reach the 12 o'clock square-to-the-target-line impact position.

90-DEGREE FOLLOW-THROUGH

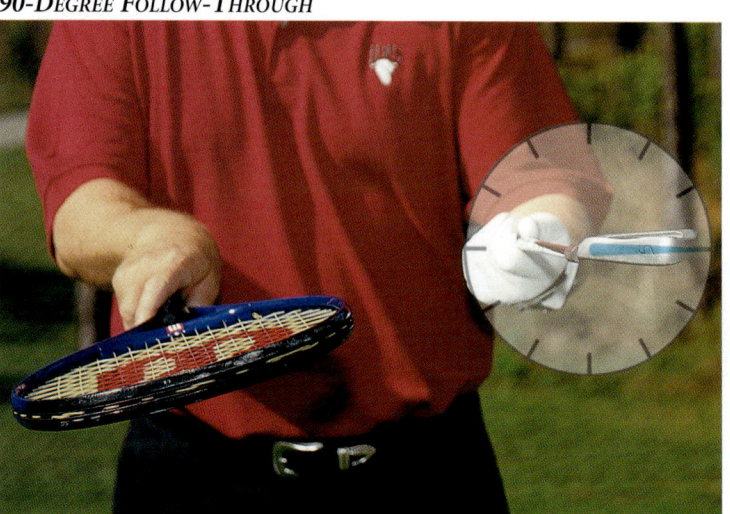

As the club swings through the ball, the arms, wrists and hands continue a counterclockwise rotation an additional 90 degrees. The checkpoint for the top of the club is:

- *3 o'clock from this view.*
- *9 o'clock from your view during the actual swing.*

Golf Myths Exposed

46

SWING CHECKPOINTS

Some of the best training aids may be lying around your house. Badminton or tennis rackets, when swung together with a golf club, provide immediate feedback on clubhead positions. The photos here show the correct *move within the move*, along with two mistakes to avoid (hooking and slicing positions).

BACKSWING

Notice the square position of both the club and racket faces at setup (1) and how that changed as the clubface rotated 90 degrees to the top of the backswing (2). At the top of this swing, the player should only be able to see the edge pointing toward the target but not the strings. Practice this at home using a mirror.

DOWNSWING/IMPACT/FOLLOW-THROUGH

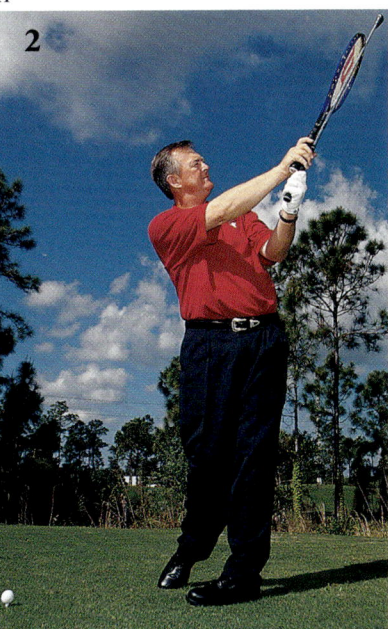

The downswing's 90-degree clubface rotation brings a square clubface to the ball at impact (1). The racket strings provide positive feedback for this clubface position that creates straight shots by sending the ball down the target line when it leaves the face. The ball can only go where the clubface points it. Continuing on to follow-through (2), another 90-degree rotation occurs, and in the mirror now you should see only the edge of the racket but not the strings.

INCORRECT POSITIONS

HOOKING POSITION

This incorrect position contributes to hooking. Instead of just the edges pointing down the target line, the racket and clubface are shut and facing the camera. The clubface will close down on the ball at impact, causing a hook.

SLICING POSITION

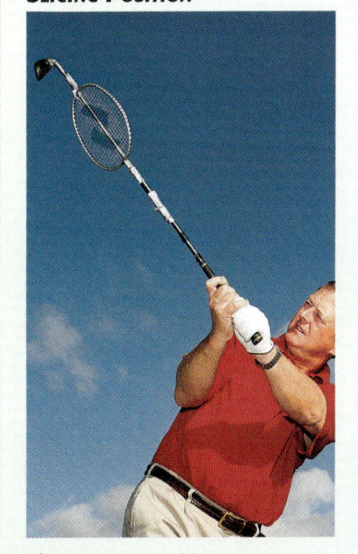

This incorrect position causes slicing. The racket and clubface are open and laid back to the target line at the backswing's top. When the clubface points to the golfer, as in this example, it will slice across the ball at impact.

SLICE-PRODUCING CHAIN REACTION

Slices are caused by the clubface applying left-to-right sidespin on the ball through the impact zone. The direction the ball takes is a combination of the direction the club is moving and where the clubface is at impact. The clubface is far more influential than the club's path on where the ball goes, but they work together to create slice sidespin.

BUILD A SOLID GAME

Understanding is the basis of lasting knowledge. Once you understand the real causes for golf-related problems, you can correct them instead of provide a brief cover-up.

In Section II we begin the process of helping you build a consistent, lifelong golf swing.

STARTING BALL FLIGHT DIRECTION	**REASON**
Pull slices: Balls that start to the left before slicing.	Clubface pointing left at impact.
Push slices: Balls that start to the right before slicing.	Clubface pointing right at impact.

1-WEAK GRIP

The V's of both hands are pointed too far to the left, creating a weak grip. This creates a clubface pointed to the right at impact, and the ball flies right.

2-BALL TOO FORWARD

Compensating for the right-side ball flight, the player puts the ball farther forward in his stance.

3-SHOULDERS POINT LEFT

The shoulders set up left of the target, compensating for the too-far-forward ball position.

4-TWISTED OPEN

The left-pointing shoulders cause the hands to twist open. The club goes back on a very flat plane.

5-SHOULDER OVERWORK

The flat plane causes the shoulders to overwork from the top. Here the clubface is incorrectly pointing forward just as the strings were (instead of the racket edge) in the incorrect move-within-the-move photo (inset).

6-LEFT CHICKEN-WING

After impact the left arm looks like a chicken wing as the club slices across the ball from right of the target line to left of the target line. This motion is also referred to as an outside-to-inside swing plane.

Why Aren't You Playing Better?

Hook-Producing Chain Reaction

Hooks are caused by the clubface applying right-to-left sidespin on the ball through the impact zone. This is caused by a combination of where the clubface is pointing and the direction the club is swinging. The direction the clubface is pointing when the ball leaves dictates the starting ball flight direction for the hook.

The Real Cure

I wouldn't want you to put Band-Aids on major wounds or apply quick fixes to major swing faults. They only cover and hide problems briefly, like makeup does.

Faster and more permanent improvement comes from understanding a problem's cause, such as this hook chain reaction. Again—Section II starts building a solid foundation for an improved lifelong game.

STARTING BALL FLIGHT DIRECTION	**REASON**
Pull hooks: Balls that start to the left before hooking.	Clubface pointing to the left at impact.
Push hooks: Balls that start to the right before hooking.	Clubface pointing to the right at impact.

1-Grip Too Strong

A too-strong grip closes the clubface during the swing. The ball starts to fly to the left at impact, the only direction it can go.

2-Ball Too Far Back

To compensate for the left-flying ball, the player places it farther back in his stance.

3-Shoulders Point Right

Shoulders inadvertently pointing to the right at address are compensating for the back-in-the-stance ball position.

4-Too Far Around Swing

The swing path follows an around-the-body path to compensate for the right-pointing shoulder position.

5-Closed Clubface

The clubface becomes closed at the top of the backswing. In the *move-within-the-move* incorrect hook photo (inset), the strings were visible, instead of the racket edge pointing down the target line, indicating a closed clubface.

6-Downswing Too Inside

The downswing path swings the club too far right.

7-Closed Clubface Through Impact

The closed clubface passes across the target line through impact, also referred to as an inside-to-outside swing plane. The hands and arms become too independent of the body through impact.

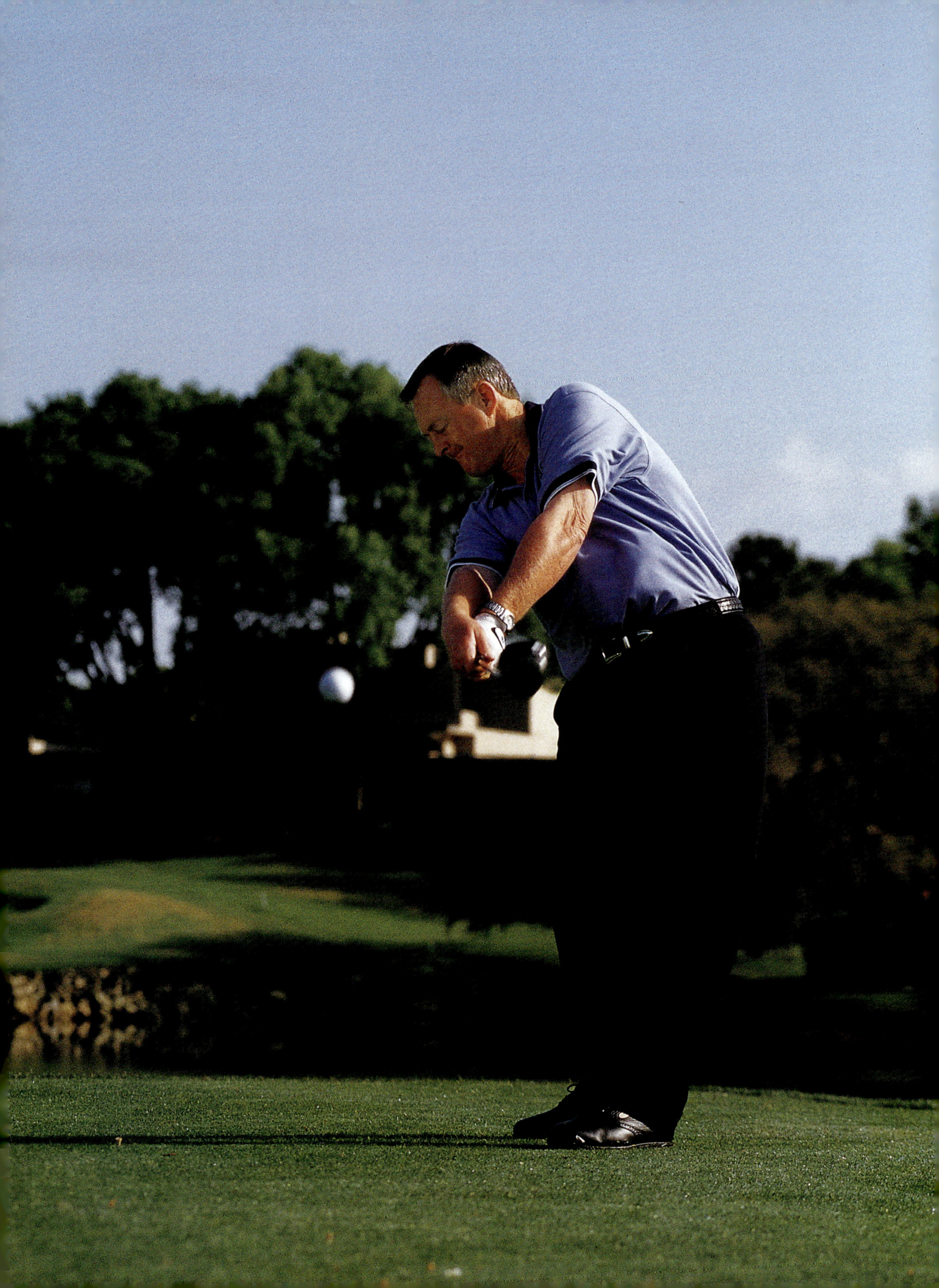

3 Instincts or Intellect: Which Is It?

When instincts take over, and they almost always will, the start of your downswing and the direction of your follow-through will always be in the opposite direction of your ball flight curvature mistake. This merits much thought!—Martin Hall

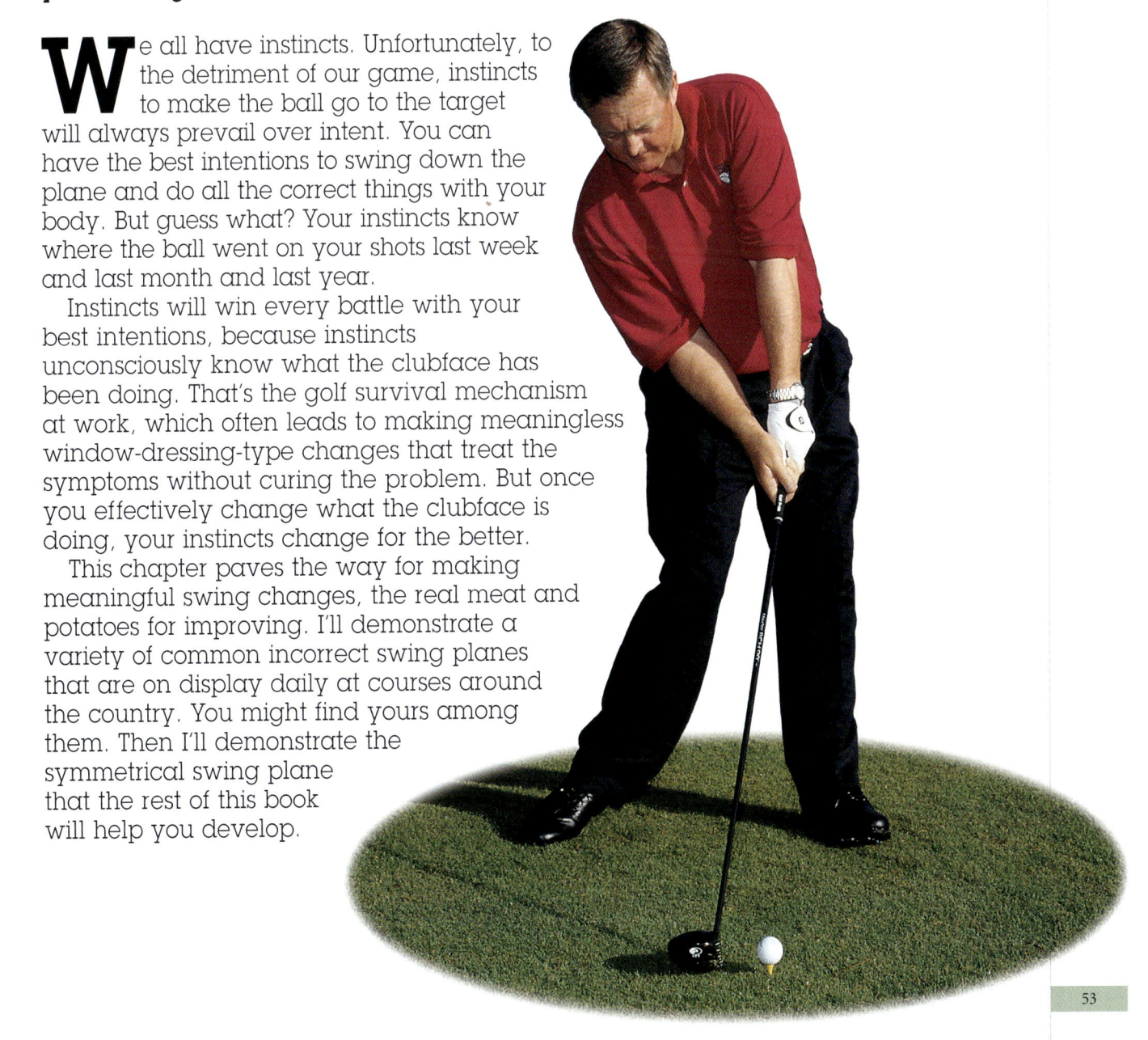

We all have instincts. Unfortunately, to the detriment of our game, instincts to make the ball go to the target will always prevail over intent. You can have the best intentions to swing down the plane and do all the correct things with your body. But guess what? Your instincts know where the ball went on your shots last week and last month and last year.

Instincts will win every battle with your best intentions, because instincts unconsciously know what the clubface has been doing. That's the golf survival mechanism at work, which often leads to making meaningless window-dressing-type changes that treat the symptoms without curing the problem. But once you effectively change what the clubface is doing, your instincts change for the better.

This chapter paves the way for making meaningful swing changes, the real meat and potatoes for improving. I'll demonstrate a variety of common incorrect swing planes that are on display daily at courses around the country. You might find yours among them. Then I'll demonstrate the symmetrical swing plane that the rest of this book will help you develop.

Opposite Instincts

Using the common slicing problem as an example, one reason for slicing the ball is the instinctive nature of swing compensations. Because the clubface is open (the problem not understood), slicers come over the top and swing to the left of the target line to try to stop the ball from ending up in right field.

This is the survival mechanism. The left side is the opposite direction of a slicer's right-side banana-curved ball flight. Trying to correct this symptom by swinging more to the left only makes the problem worse and creates a variety of pulled shots to the left or even bigger slices, depending on the clubface position at impact.

Each of the following swing misconceptions are also based on good intentions. But when instincts take over—as they always will, fed by the fuel of misunderstanding—performance will get worse instead of better. Studying these swing misconceptions provides the understanding to shift your swing to the correct plane with the correct clubface angle. This is the only way to consistently lower your scores.

Meat and Potatoes Swing Changes

Unhappy with your ball flight? Then change one of three things you do while swinging the club. Working on anything other than these three things means not working on anything that really will make a difference. The three are:

1 - Change the clubface position at impact.

2 - Change the direction in which the club is moving.

3 - Change where you hit the ball on the clubface.

Misconception #1: Swing Too Upright

Problem
Golfers, whose swings are seen in these photos, have the misconception that to hit the ball straight they must swing the club back and down along a straight line.

Truth
Improvement comes from understanding that golf swings cannot have any straight lines, because the club follows a tilted oval. The clubhead is always moving along a curved path.

Upright swings are easy to spot with the club set straight up in the air on the backswing (1). The golfer is lucky if he doesn't knock himself out with his right arm during this follow-through (2).

Misconception #2: Swing Too Flat

Problem
Golfers with flat swings have fallen prey to the turn, turn, turn misconception, and are in fact turning too much. The club does not follow the correct plane, so balance suffers.

Truth
Improvement comes from understanding that more is not always better, and that's especially true with the backswing pivot. Turn only enough to put the club on the correct swing arc.

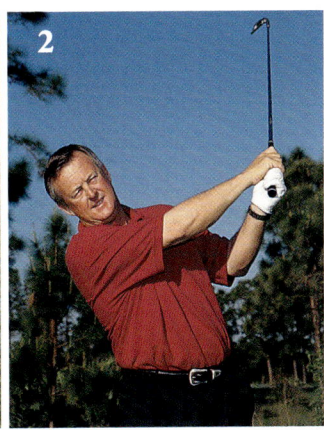

This incorrect flat position (1) should be called the back of the backswing instead of the top of the backswing. Weak follow-throughs from this incorrect plane (2) reveal the lack of power generated by the swing.

Misconception #3: The Misguided Distance Swing Plane

Problem
This one is easy to spot by the flayed elbows. This golfer is trying to produce more clubhead speed regardless of the cost to his swing plane. He has lost his elbow structure in trying so hard and so incorrectly.

Truth
Improvement comes by understanding that maintaining structure plays an integral part in producing more clubhead speed to increase your distance. Maintaining this structure during the correct order of motion as you coil and uncoil produces consistently longer and more accurate shots.

Martin demonstrates an incorrect swing plane (1 and 2) caused by losing elbow structure while trying to get the clubhead back farther. Proper structure creates swing speed.

For comparative purposes see how John Daly (3) swings past parallel with his club yet keeps the correct structure with his left arm, hands and wrists at the end of his backswing. Daly's swing speed can climb to 140 miles per hour in only a fraction of a second on the downswing.

Instincts or Intellect: Which Is It?

55

Misconception #4: Swing Goes Too Low to Too High

Problem

Trying to cover up other real swing problems, this golfer now has the problem of having the club approach the ball too shallow and rising too high after impact. Fat or thin shots are the usual results.

Truth

Improvement comes from understanding that good golf swings have a beautiful sense of symmetry to them. Backswings and follow-throughs match, proving that the club has followed the correct swing path through the ball.

Misconception #5: Swing Path Too High to Too Low

Problem

Trying to artificially extend the swing arc is one reason for this golfer taking the club back too high. An angle of attack that is too high on the approach and takes big divots after the ball is hit are the telltale signs of this problem. Lots of pulled shots to the left with the short iron is another sign.

Truth

Improvement comes from understanding that an efficient swing is a balanced swing. You can't be high on one end and low on the other. Swing arcs must have symmetry by following the tilted oval and not deviating from it with incorrect instinctive compensations.

Martin demonstrates the incorrect low-to-high swing plane responsible for a variety of fat or thin shots along with pushes and hooks. Overall swing symmetry is out of whack as the hands are low (1) on the backswing but high on the follow-through (4). As a result, the approach to the ball is too shallow (2) and too high past impact (3).

Martin demonstrates the incorrect high-to-low swing plane, creating an attack angle that brings the club down to the ball along a steep angle, causing deep divots after impact and pulled shots.

This swing lacks symmetry as the backswing is high (1) while the follow-through is low (4). Consequently, the club approaches the ball too steeply (2) and stays too low to the ground (3) following impact.

Instincts or Intellect: Which Is It?

57

Symmetrical Swing Plane
The One and Only Truth

Compare the correct swing plane sequence (below) to the ones on pages 56 and 57. Notice here how the hand positions match at the top of my backswing and follow-through, and how the club arrives at the ball following the correct approach path.

Compared to the other photos showing the swing plane misconceptions, notice how my backswing and follow-through hand positions match. This swing arc is symmetrical and the bottom of the swing arc is where the clubhead arrives at the ball square to the target line (3) and continues along the correct arc past impact (4). A key checkpoint for any golf swing (1) features the club shaft parallel to the target line on the backswing when it is parallel to the ground. This is one of five times the shaft must be parallel in your swing; we'll discuss those five occurrences in Chapter 4.

NO CONCEPT/NO CHANCE

If you have no concept as to what the golf swing really entails, then regrettably you have no chance to succeed. This leads to frustration because the bottom line is you don't really know how to get better.

Frustration may best be defined as **expectation minus reality.** Unfortunately, some golfers combine this with unrealistic expectations about what the status of their game *should* be. *Should* is a horrible word when used as: I *should* have been able to do this. One instructor I know tells his students, "Don't *should* all over yourselves."

Should creates both muscular and mental tension. It creates mental interference and you get yourself into a mess. When you're trying to play your best on the golf course, that wretched word *should* gets your emotions running away from you, gets your heartbeat going and gets your palms sweating, none of which helps you play better golf. Controlling your emotions might be just as important as controlling your swing plane when it comes to playing well under pressure!

All the *shoulds* add mental pressure and can very easily disrupt your golf swing. Sports psychologist Jim Leohr suggests having a script to follow so that inevitably when you hit bad shots you have a response such as, "Hmmm, that's interesting," instead of beating yourself up with, "You dirty rotten @#&*!" Having a script or pet phrase can keep you on an emotionally level keel.

Eddy Merrins, the esteemed former golf coach at UCLA, recommends "that after every shot you don't care for, say to yourself, 'So what! So it went in the water—no big deal.'" While some people might think this suggests you are not trying hard enough, the reality is that we often play better golf by **trying a little less,** and all this *should*-linked mental pressure we put on ourselves makes us try too hard, negatively affecting our performance levels.

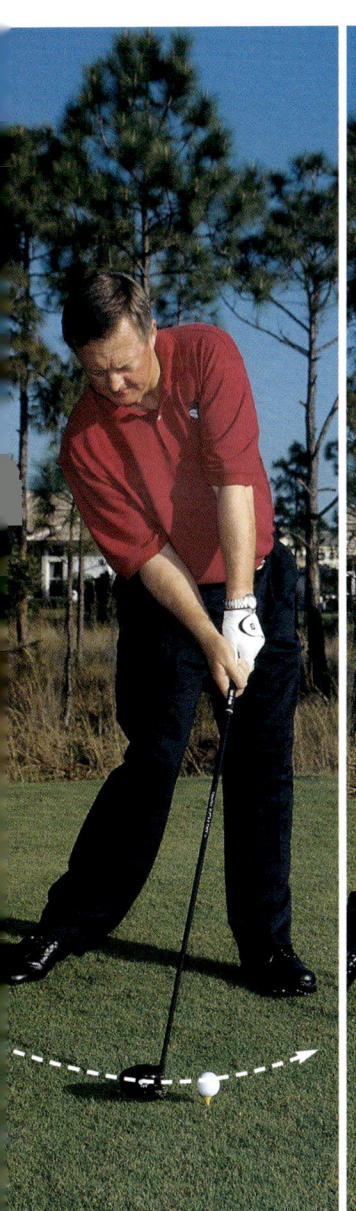

'Plane' Simple Geometry

If I ever become Commissioner of Golf for the planet Earth, I would decree that everyone who played golf would have their own personal swing plane board for a training aid. Golfers would then have a basis for understanding golf's geometry. Follow the photos below for a preview of what your swing will look like after reading and using the drills in Chapter 4.

Using a PVC swing plane training aid, Martin demonstrates the correct tilted oval swing plane.

1-Setup

For demonstration purposes, the clubface is set up square to the target line. In actuality, the only time great players' clubfaces are square is when the ball leaves the face.

2-Takeaway

Notice how the clubface is looking at the ball as it goes up the plane.

3-Waist-High Parallel

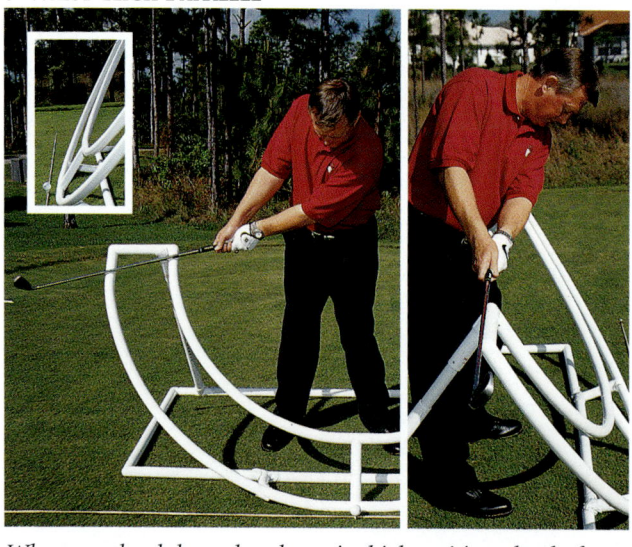

Whenever the club reaches the waist-high position, the shaft should be parallel to the line. To hit a straight shot, the club must return to this position on the downswing, and to a matching one when it reaches waist high after impact. Chapter 4 shows you how to get your club shaft parallel to the target line five times during your swing.

4-Backswing Continuation

With a dowel placed in the butt of the club for illustration purposes, you can easily see how the club remains on the tilted oval plane after the head leaves the training aid. Notice the triangle formed by my shoulders, arms and hands.

PRACTICE SWINGS DON'T TELL YOU EVERYTHING

The noted instructor John Jacobs gave a wonderful answer to his students whenever he heard them say, "I make great practice swings. I'm sure that if I hit the ball with my practice swing, the shot would be good." To that Jacobs would jokingly reply, "You've got no proof of that!"

We now have computers that can show where the clubface is at impact when hitting a ball or taking a practice swing. What we find is that these people who are taking what they feel are wonderful practice swings, are often arriving at the ball with the clubface as much as 15 to 20 degrees open.

The only way you can really judge the true state of your swing is by the direction the ball flies when you hit it. Remember that the ball can **only go** in the direction the clubface is pointing at impact. By that measure you'll know immediately how good your swing really is.

5-Downswing

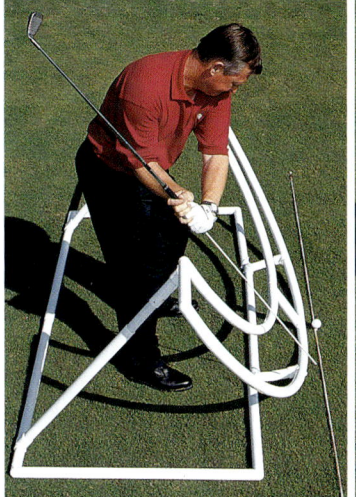

Important in these photos, follow the clubhead's path toward the ball in relation to the target line. Notice that the path does not stray from the tilted oval, and the clubface is once again looking at the ball. At no time will the clubhead pass over the target line or approach the ball along a swing path any farther inside than what you see here.

6-Impact

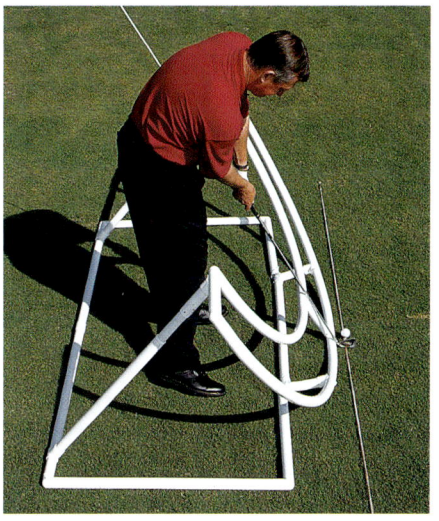

Following along the correct swing plane brings the club back to the ball, square to the target line. The only time the ball will fly along this line is if the clubface is pointing to the target when the ball leaves.

7-Downswing Continuation and Follow-Through

Checking the clubhead and shaft positions along with my body positions shows how the club stays on plane. The triangle of my shoulders, arms and hands keeps the butt of the club in the correct position all the way through.

Instincts or Intellect: Which Is It?

Sweet Spot

The entire purpose of the golf swing is mating the sweet spot of the club to the center of the ball at impact. The farther away that impact occurs from these two spots, the less distance you will get.

Now consider the difficulty in doing this. The golf club accelerates faster in the same fractional amount of elapsed time than a supersonic jet fighter, and you must cause two spots to meet perfectly. There is only one way to do this consistently: train your swing to correctly follow a consistent swing plane.

Are You Hitting the Sweet Spot?

You can achieve consistent club distances only if you hit the ball on the sweet spot. Apply decals or powder paint (available through golf specialty stores) to your clubface to help you see how close to the sweet spot you're hitting the ball. Here are three examples.

Martin Hall shows off his sweet spot hit.

Sweet Spot Hit

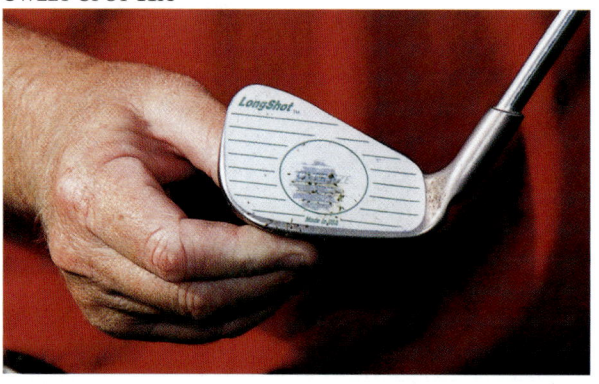

This ball impacted the face in the middle of the sweet spot. If this is your report card, you have graduated to accurate yardage assignments for each club.

Heel Hit

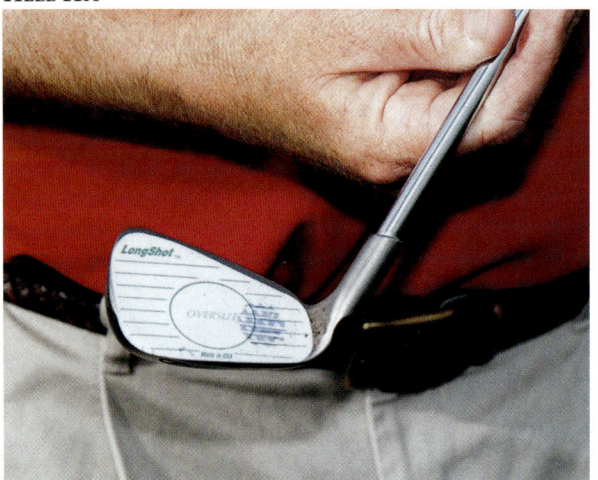

If you see this heel hit on your clubface, your shot patterns are usually to the left or a shank to the right or left. Heel hits close the clubface down at impact. Hitting the ball on the heel can be a result of:

- *Standing too close to the ball at address.*

- *Swinging inside to out.*

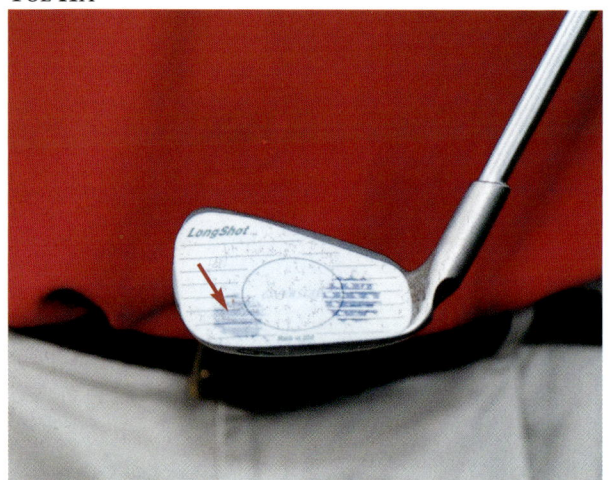

Toe Hit

Here the same decal shows the difference between the previously mentioned heel hit and a toe hit (arrow). Hitting it on the toe opens the clubface, usually sending the ball to the right. The reasons can include:

- *Standing too far away from the ball at address.*

- *Swinging outside to in.*

SWING PLANE SWEET SPOT DRILL

Swing plane accuracy controls shot distance and accuracy. It's all-important once you are in middle iron territory. This outstanding drill maintains swing plane perfection. The best part is, you can do this drill in your backyard, keeping your swing sharp.

Ideally, the club and ball should meet on the iron's sweet spot instead of the toe or heel. Substituting three tees for your ball places the emphasis on swinging through a gate as opposed to hitting an object.

1- FIND THE SWEET SPOT

Use a red tee to simulate the ball. Place the tee in the ground about halfway up the center of the clubface.

2- TOE GATE

Place a white tee just off the toe of your clubface.

3- HEEL GATE

Place another white tee at an angle about an inch outside of the clubface's heel. You now have a gate to swing through. The key is to only hit the red tee.

4- SWEET SPOT IMPACT

Swinging through the gate, the clubface only hit the red tee, resulting in an accurate middle iron swing. The next two photos are examples of mishits, resulting in off-target shots.

TOE HITS TEE—HEEL HITS BALL

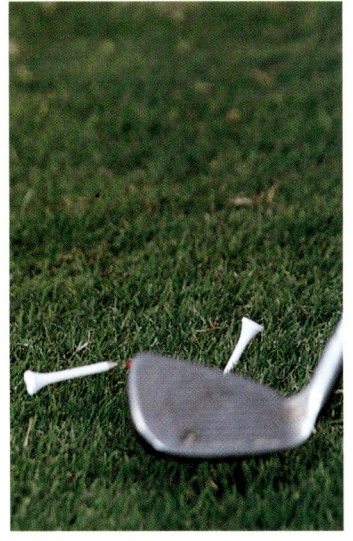

On this swing the toe incorrectly hit the outside tee. This would lead to an incorrect hit in the heel. This closes the clubface, sending the ball off target to the left.

HEEL HITS TEE—TOE HITS BALL

Knocking the inside tee out of the ground indicates the ball would have been hit with the toe of the club. This opens the clubface, sending the ball off target to the right.

Instincts or Intellect: Which Is It?

SECTION II
VEGETABLES BEFORE DESSERT

My dear mom always said you must eat your vegetables or get no dessert. She knew greens were good for us. Still, no one liked eating their vegetables. But everybody loved eating dessert. Maybe we all need a mother to help us play better golf, because this same basic principle still applies.

To become better golfers, we all need to do the things we perceive to be boring or unimportant. As a golfer, you'll never perform any better than your fundamental motion. The vegetables of golf really are working on those fundamentals and developing the understanding of how to first have a very high-quality half-swing before moving on to a full swing.

Students sometimes ask, "How come I can't hit a 3-wood off a downhill lie?" The answer may be because they also can't hit a quality 50-yard chip. Learn to do the right thing in slow motion, with short swings, and then gradually build up to full swings using your newly improved swing mechanics.

In this section, let's make sure you develop a really good understanding of the golf swing. Let's make sure you know how to stand, how to start the swing back and how to bring it down. Let's make sure you understand why golf balls go where they go when they go off line. Eat these vegetables and you'll savor the dessert of lower scores that await.

IN THIS SECTION

BUILDING A BALANCED GOLF SWING

- Tension is Golf's #1 Enemy
- Top Ten Keys
- Grip Checks
- Grip Pressure Check
- Perfect Posture
- Ball Position
- Ball Flight Diagnosis
- A Pro's Balance
- Dynamic Balance
- Weight Check

BACKSWING

- Golf's Basic Geometry
- Rhythm Swing Check
- Martin's Drills for an On-Plane Backswing
- Windup Resistance
- Takeaway
- Preset Wrist
- Keep Hands Low
- Clubface Looks at Ball
- Left Arm Check
- Shadow Coil

TRANSITION

- Avoiding the Hit Impulse
- Balanced Transition
- Engine and Caboose
- Martin's Transition Drills
- Correct Order of Movement
- Smooth Acceleration
- Maintain the Tension Drill
- Shaft/Shoulder Relationship

DOWNSWING TO IMPACT

- Swing Club Toward Target
- Ball Leaves Square to Target Line
- Keys to Power Golf
- Solid Hits
- Martin's Drills
- Elbow Push
- Transfer Energy Down Shaft
- Drag Shaft Through Hitting Zone

PAST IMPACT TO FINISH

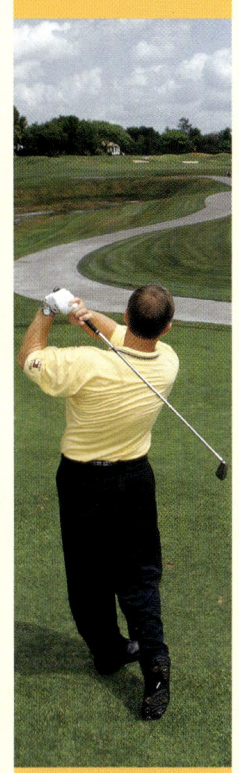

- Straight Arms After Impact
- Clubhead Rotation
- Martin's Drills
- Toss the Water
- Johnny Miller Recoil Drills
- Elbows Down
- Gardner Dickinson Drill
- Compression Drill

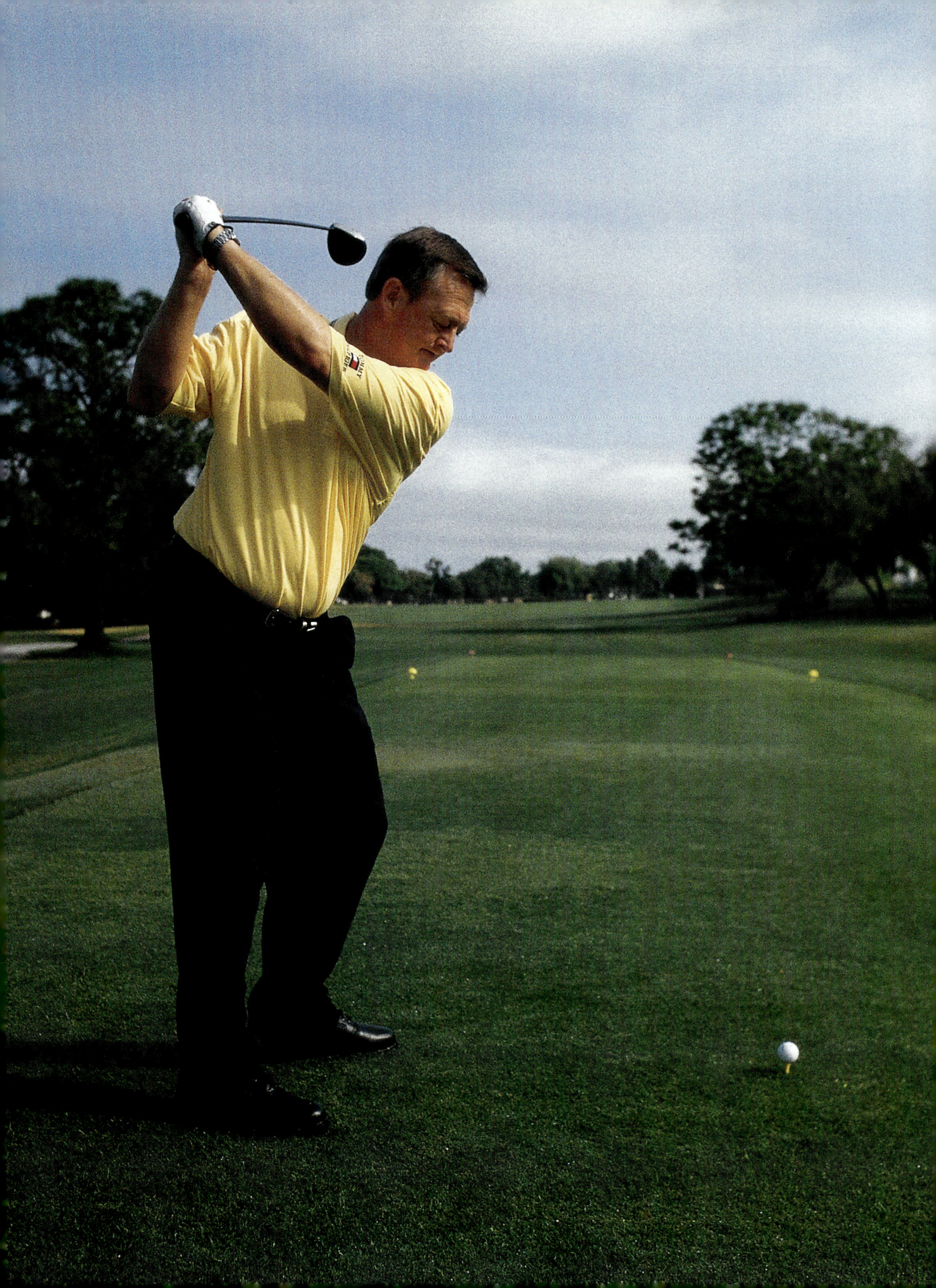

4 Building a Balanced Golf Swing

Balance is not just holding your finish position. Balance means not being out of position during your golf swing so you can give yourself the best chance to smack that ball with a square face in the middle of the clubhead.—Martin Hall

The successful *on-plane full swing* is like a big, sweet, tasty dessert, sitting there waiting with whipped cream and chocolate sauce and a big cherry on top. But before you can get to this ultimate reward and savor every well-deserved spoonful, you need some good hearty vegetables (basic fundamentals) for proper nourishment. How should you start? To begin, understand that golf swings are based on geometry.

You must develop repeatable specialized skills for consistently propelling the club around a tilted plane with the objective of squaring the clubface to the target line at impact. These are the *vegetable* skills, but I promise that mastering these vital fundamentals will not be tedious or boring or waste your time once you get to the course.

You can practice many of these fundamentals at home with simple, entertaining drills. The fast track to improvement requires that you understand the role of each skill and its importance to the success of your swing. Just like a speeding train, it's vital that the engine leads, not the caboose. Let's begin by using my all-time Top 10 List of Hits—the fundamentals for playing better golf.

Martin's Top 10 Hits

Working with golfers of differing skill levels, I've found the best way to improve is to place the emphasis on only those things that contribute to developing square-to-the-line clubface positions.

If all your work on mechanics is not geared toward changing incorrect face positions, then, to be honest, you are really wasting your time. Here are the fundamentals that affect clubface positions the most.

1 - Grip

2 - Ball Position

3 - Balanced Posture

4 - Balance

5 - Plane

6 - Pivot

7 - Clubface at checkpoints in swing

8 - Tempo

9 - Timing

10 - Rhythm

Tension: Golf's Number 1 Enemy

Swing mistakes may not be the sole reason a ball goes off line. Sometimes even excellent players have trouble finding the true culprit when evaluating what went wrong with their shots. Golf's public enemy No. 1 may be at work. A little bit of tension in the shoulders, neck or hands, for example, can prevent the blade from squaring up or can close it down too soon. Once you develop good form, then tension becomes an even bigger issue.

Once you incorporate the Top 10 Hits list into your swing mechanics and produce golf swings that are relatively tension-free, you are on your way toward becoming a very good player. But tension will negate all the good work of the Top 10 if you let it.

Eliminate Tension

Partners Club President Tom Lehman realizes that tension tends to build up in his shoulders and neck. To prevent this, Tom incorporates a neck stretch as part of his pre-shot routine. Tension is a swing inhibitor and must be prevented from destroying all the good fundamentals.

GRIP

Gripping the club correctly is the single most important thing any golfer can do to change clubface position at impact. Most golf problems stem from leaving the clubface open as the ball leaves, and incorrect hand positions are a big part of the reason that this occurs.

Better players will check their grips first before making any radical swing changes. It's sort of like being a Ferrari mechanic who tunes the high-performance engines, making only slight tweaks in the settings instead of taking a sledgehammer and bashing away.

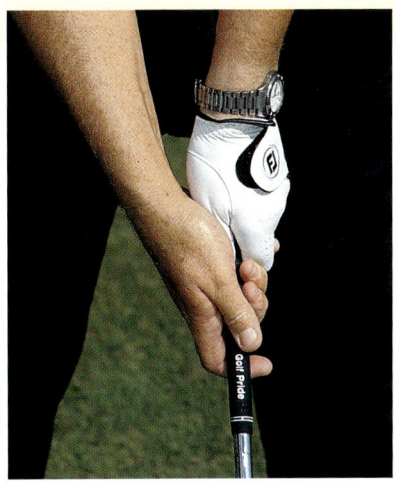

A good grip contributes to squaring the clubface at impact.

GRIP CHECKS

Here are two good ways to check your grip as you practice. Even though a grip becomes second nature and comfortable, it's always important to make sure that what feels correct *really* is.

LEFT THUMB ON THE SIDE

Checking the left thumb position is your first grip check. Your left thumb should always be slightly on the side of the grip instead of right down the center of the shaft.

RIGHT HAND SWINGS BACK

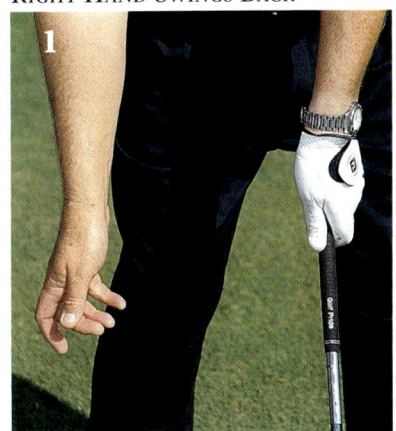

The second grip check is the right hand position. By taking the right hand off the club, allowing gravity to swing the hand to the side (1), it should return to the side of the club every time (2).

BAD EXAMPLE

If your right hand (1) is too far under the club—the overly strong position—it will fall toward your right leg (2). Just the opposite will take place if the right hand is more on the top of the club—weak grip position—because it will gravitate outward.

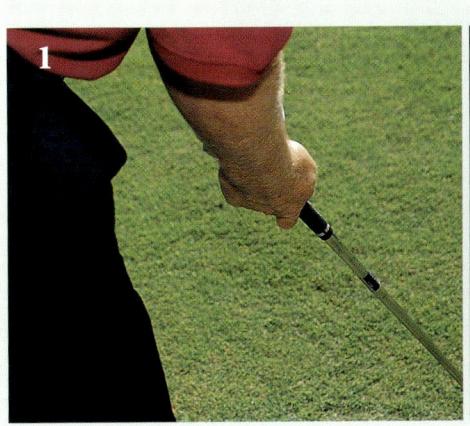

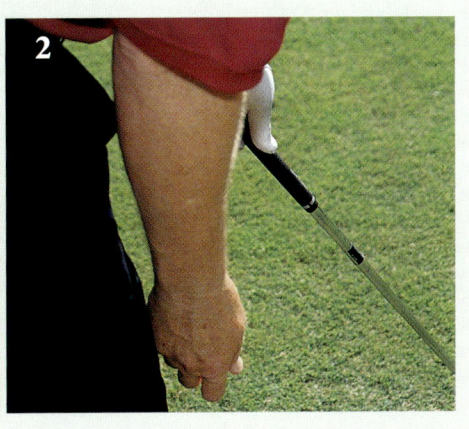

Building a Balanced Golf Swing

69

Grip-Friendly Helpers

Nearly all the golfers I've taught over the years are what I call *palm grippers*, who incorrectly hold the club solely in the palm of their hands. This problem is quickly overcome once you think more in terms of making sure the *fleshy part of the left hand* sits on top of the handle. That automatically places the club sufficiently in your fingers.

The Role of the Left Hand

The left hand controls the clubface, and it's vitally important to position it properly. The way your left hand hangs naturally is how it should go onto the golf club.

Pocket Check

Try this grip-friendly method to properly position your left hand on the club. Grip your club with your left hand resting by your trouser pocket.

Fleshy Part on Top

Placing the fleshy part of the left hand on top of the grip correctly positions the club across your open fingers for support.

Left Hand Check

It's always a good idea to verify you are doing things correctly, so here's a left hand grip check. If you are correctly gripping the club with your fingers, you should be able to place a tee between the top of the shaft and the base of the palm pad. Check your left thumb position, making sure it's on the right side of the shaft.

Watching Your Tees and V's

Your hands must be positioned where they are most likely to return the clubface square at impact. Tees placed in the V's formed by both hands should point between your right shoulder and chin but more toward your right shoulder.

Square Face Grip

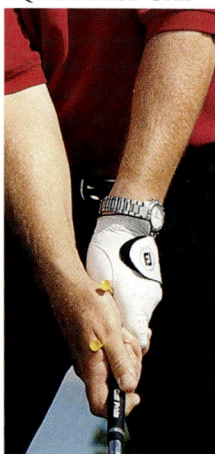

This grip position enhances your ability to return the clubface square to the ball at impact.

Hooker's Grip

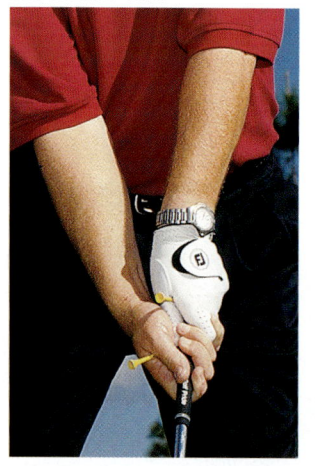

When the tees are pointed to the right of the shoulder, hooks are the result. Notice how the right hand is under the club instead of on the side.

Slicer's Grip

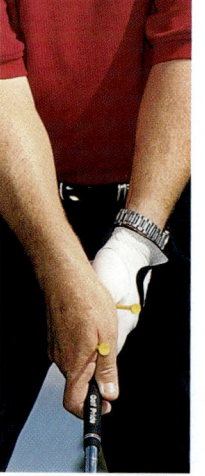

When the tees are pointed toward the left shoulder, slices are the result. This is the classic mistake position that creates a clubface that points to the right of the target line (open) at impact. Notice how the right hand is on top of the club instead of to the side.

Point the Tees to 1 o'clock

As a final grip check, the tees placed in the V's formed by both hands should point to 1 o'clock. Try thinking in terms of visual clock positions instead of strong or weak.

OVERLAP OR INTERLOCK?

This is one area where the choice depends on which you prefer. Higher handicap golfers seem to prefer using a mutilated hybrid version of either the interlock or overlap grips. Players like Tiger Woods, John Daly and Jack Nicklaus all prefer to interlock the index finger of the left hand with the pinkie of the right hand. But amateur golfers seem to mess this one up the most. Instead of inter*lock*, I'd call their hybrid mutilation inter*loose*.

INTERLOCK CORRECTLY

INTERLOOSE

Be sure to lock your interlock grip! Your fingers should be closed without any gaps between the hands.

Can you see why I refer to this incorrect interlock grip as interloose*? The space between the fingers is an incorrect interpretation of the grip that Tiger uses so successfully.*

INTERLOCK GRIP CHECK

Checking your interlock grip periodically for proper hand placement makes good sense. All your fundamentals, even those you take for granted, should be constantly checked, or your swing plane will suffer. For example, how you grip the club may be the single most important thing you do to ensure a square clubface. But how often have you checked your grip in the past?

Building a Balanced Golf Swing

71

Thumb Position: Distance or Accuracy

The left thumb length you leave on the club can help increase your distance or increase your accuracy. A *short left thumb* that extends down the shaft, equal to the forefinger, allows you to have more wrist action, which in turn creates additional speed coming through. A *longer left thumb* position has the opposite effect, tightening up the wrists and the forearm, which promotes additional accuracy. The choice is yours, depending on the situation.

More Distance = Shorter Thumb

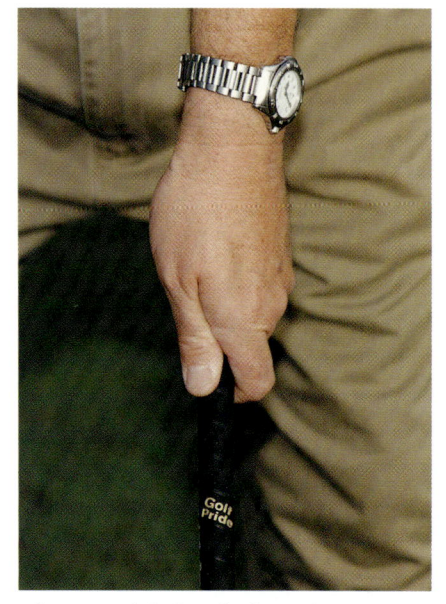

Place your left thumb about the same distance down the shaft as your forefinger. Notice, however, that the thumb is still on the right side of the shaft.

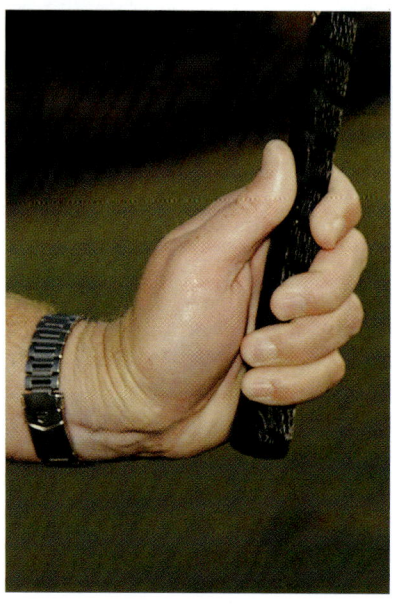

Shorter left thumb positions encourage more wrist flexibility, which promotes more speed in your swing for additional distance.

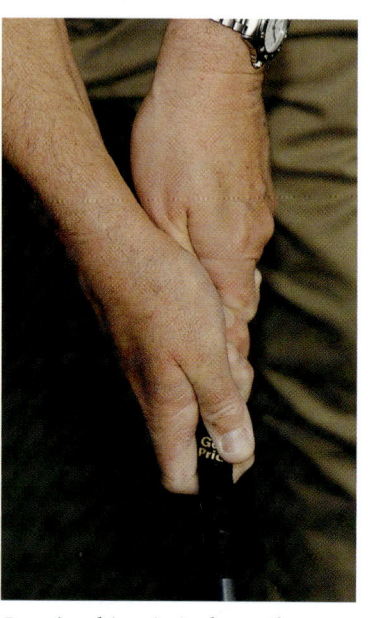

Practice this grip in front of a mirror. You should not see the left thumb "peeking out" as you look at the grip.

More Accuracy = Longer Thumb

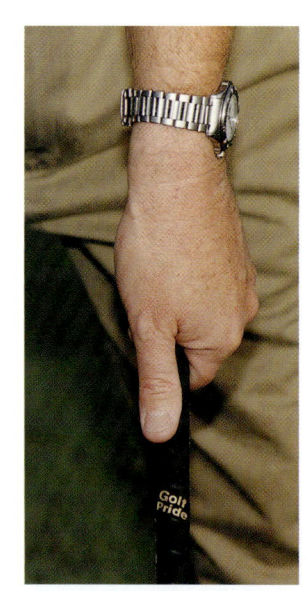

Place your left thumb so that it extends down the right side of the shaft.

Longer left thumb positions limit the amount of wrist hinge during the swing. Some swing speed may be lost, but accuracy improves.

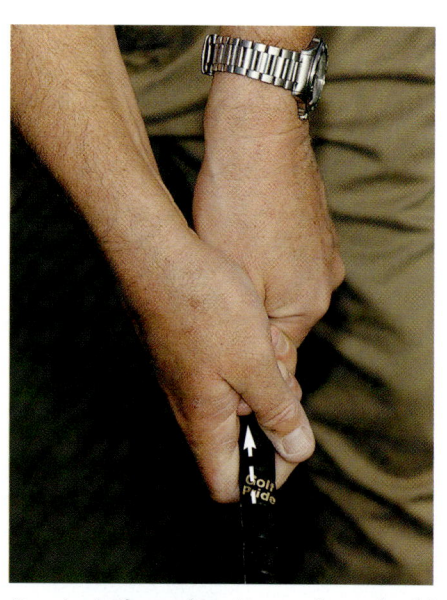

Practice in front of a mirror and you should see the thumb "peeking out" (arrow) if the thumb is extended down the grip.

A Useful Grip Thought

Eliminate all air pockets as you grip the club. Grip pressure should be light but not loose. Davis Love was an outstanding teacher (his son is PGA TOUR professional Davis Love III), and I like to use this bit of advice he gave his students regarding hand position.

"Visualize smearing the handle of your club with sticky glue, and place your hands on the grip very carefully, feeling you are getting all the air pockets out for a perfect fit."

A technique I use while teaching my students is to grab the club and try to move it. How tightly they hold the club is astounding. Even if they set up with loose grip pressure, many tighten up when they get halfway back.

Too much grip pressure affects clubface behavior during the swing. You can still make a good-looking swing, but gripping the club too tightly negatively affects the swing arc on which the clubface should be closing prior to impact. This can be responsible for a right-pointing (open) clubface as the ball leaves it.

Constant Grip Pressure

Don't make the mistake of thinking that grip pressure only matters when you set up to the ball. The best players in the game have a constant grip pressure all through their motion.

Grip Pressure Check

Grip pressure extends beyond just your hands. Another good check is extending the club and rotating it in small circles to see how the grip pressure is affecting the wrists and elbows.

Hold your club out in front and make some small circles, first to the left, then to the right. Your wrists should be as relaxed as possible. A good mental image is to think of your hands as clamps while your wrists are free.

If Your Grip Slips

If the club moves in your hands at impact, the reason may not be that you are gripping it too lightly. It's more likely that you are striking the ball on the toe or heel of the club instead of the center or sweet spot.

Building a Balanced Golf Swing

Ball Position

In the setup, ball position and grip are the two elements that most influence the ball's flight direction.

> ### Swaying Changes Ball Position
>
> Your clubface should only square up at the bottom of the swing arc. But this position will vary if you sway during your swing. For example, swaying forward with the upper body has the effect of moving the ball back in your stance as much as six inches.
>
> That's why someone who sways, yet correctly sets up with the ball off the left heel, wonders why the ball flight pushed to the right. The reason: A ball back in your stance meets a clubface that is pointing to the right at impact.

The clubface only *looks at the target* for a fraction of a second at impact, so you must have the ball positioned in that exact spot if you want to hit a straight shot. Because we stand to the side of the ball, geometrically the club travels back, up and in along a tilted swing arc, never following a straight line. There is nothing you can do to change this basic rule as you work to improve.

If you ever hear anyone—including television analysts—say that a player is so good because they can go down the line longer or keep the clubface square longer, give a one-word response: Rubbish!

What really happens is that the best players in the world have the clubface square to the target line more often than others at impact. There is a tremendous amount of timing involved to reach the squared position, similar to the swinging doors of a saloon in an old Western movie. Each swinging door, like the swinging clubface, follows an arc as it swings in and out. The square position occurs only briefly as both swing through.

That one brief moment when the doors reach the perfect closed position (the clubface impacts the ball) is the only moment that really counts. And as you'll see in Chapter 7, this is one you have no control over at the exact moment when this occurs.

Ball Flight Diagnosis

Ball Flight	Diagnosis	Check
Shots go to the right.	Clubface looking to the right at impact.	Check your grip and the ball position. Is ball position too far back in your stance?
Shots go to the left.	Clubface looking to the left at impact.	Check your grip and the ball position. Is ball position too far forward in your stance?

Golf Myths Exposed

Correct Ball Position

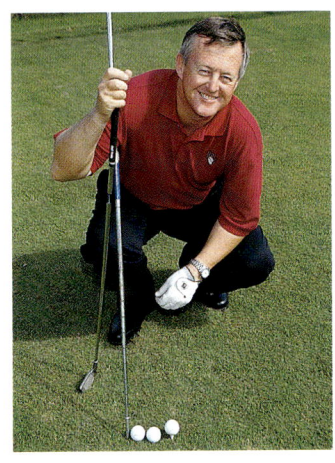

The ball should be placed at the bottom of the swing arc of each type of club. Different length shafts dictate different ball positions. The bottom of the arc for longer clubs, such as drivers, is farther forward in the stance than it is for shorter clubs.

Martin uses a long shaft to demonstrate three correct ball positions.

Working the Ball Positions

If someone tells you to position the ball back in the stance when you want to hit a draw (controlled right-to-left ball flight), that sometimes works. The theory is that the club impacts the ball while swinging to the right and will curve the ball around. But I have a suggestion that offers more consistency.

Play a big draw off the tee by first aiming to the right of the target, and position the ball farther forward in your stance. With the ball up front, it gives the clubface more time to close. I've had more success shaping a draw doing it this way.

When you want to hit a fade, try an opposite tack. First aim to the left of the target and then position the ball farther back in your stance.

Driving

I placed a long shaft by my left ear for a reference point. Ideally the best ball position for driving is under your left armpit.

Middle Irons

For the middle irons, the best ball position is one ball length back in the stance, between the left armpit and left ear.

Short Irons

The short iron ball position is another ball length back to a position under the left ear.

Building a Balanced Golf Swing

75

Drill

Ball Position Drill

Backyard Ball Position Drill

To be honest, there is no foolproof way to set up to the correct ball position every time. Having said that, try this excellent drill to train your instincts correctly. This drill is best done in your backyard where you can take the time to repeatedly position the ball as correctly as possible. This will soon become familiar and comfortable, and begins building your confidence for establishing your setup position.

1-Set Up the Drill

Stretch two pieces of rope so they form a right angle. The horizontal line is the target line and the vertical is for your left foot position.

2-Right Foot Placement

After teeing a ball where the ropes intersect, walk toward the line pigeon-toed. Touch your right foot to the line (pigeon-toed) (inset), which positions your upper body correctly.

3-Square Club Placement

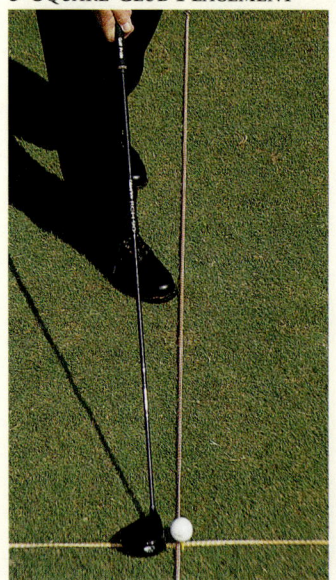

Place the club behind the ball so that it points down the target line.

4-Left Foot Placement

Place your left foot across the line, which still keeps your upper body in position.

5-Adjust the Width

Keeping your left heel touching the line, adjust the width of your stance by moving your right foot.

Balanced Posture

Watch someone lose their balance when they slip. The very first thing they do—another survival mechanism—is start moving their arms wildly, struggling to recapture their balance. Now think about which parts of the body hold and swing the club? Your arms and hands!

Lose some degree of balance during your swing, and the body makes an involuntary survival motion—using the hands and arms—to recapture it, but taking the club off the swing plane in the process.

If your posture doesn't maintain balance all through the golf swing, you will never be consistent. Over the years you've undoubtedly read dozens of swing tips and articles dealing with the importance of setting the correct posture angles at setup. But did any of that information ever mention how vital it is to maintain balance all the way through your swing?

Correct posture is one of Martin Hall's Top 10 Hits for balanced swings.

A Pro's Swing Balance

The need for balance during your golf swing can't be stressed enough. Scott McCarron, one of the PGA TOUR'S statistical driving leaders, realized early in his career that he needed to develop a way to practice his balance during the swing. McCarron used a gymnastics balance-beam technique to turn himself into one of golf's top players.

Scott's "beam" is a Styrofoam log, and standing on it shoeless, he makes full swings with a heavy club while maintaining his balance thoughout the swing. Posture is what creates his balance.

PGA TOUR professional Scott McCarron uses a Styrofoam log to practice his balanced swing shoeless. McCarron, at 5'10" and 165 pounds, annually ranks among the top five in driving distance on the PGA TOUR.

Scott McCarron's Balance Beam Drill

Standing barefoot (or in socks as seen here) and using a heavy club training aid, Scott McCarron makes 20 swings, beginning with a slow tempo. He starts slow to feel all the positions of the swing and to detect if he begins to get out of balance any place along the way. Smoothness is the key, since any needless motion or maneuver causes golfers to lose balance. Losing your balance means losing your swing plane, too!

Starting from a balanced posture position (1, 2), Scott bends from the hips, flexes his knees and sticks his tailbone out a bit. Being shoeless helps him gain the maximum feeling of his shifting weight and balance points.

As he smoothly continues to the top of his backswing (4, 5), his dynamic balance adjusts for the shifting weight. McCarron's posture is responsible for his ability to maintain his balance as he swings down and through impact (6) all the way to a balanced follow-through. (8, 9).

Two other important swing-check balance positions are also seen here—the hip-high shaft positions. Later we'll cover the importance of having the shaft parallel to the target line anytime it's in the waist-high position. During the backswing (3) and past impact (7), when McCarron's club reaches the waist-high positions, notice that the club is parallel to his target line even in this practice drill.

Golf Myths Exposed

78

SET UP IN BALANCE

Try this three-step tip for always setting up in balance.

1 - Take a bow.

2 - Bend your knees.

3 - Stick your butt out.

BALANCE POSTURE CHECK

Use two old shafts stuck together to provide a simple-to-use posture check, or have a friend hold a long pole in the same position you see here.

Your posture is balanced if you can draw a line from the top of the spine downward that just touches the inside of the right elbow and the tip of the knees, and then continues down into the balls of your feet.

OUT OF BALANCE POSTURE #1

This upright position will not be able to support your club swinging along the correct plane. Compare the balance points with those seen in the "correct" photo.

OUT OF BALANCE POSTURE #2

This bent-over position has the balance line going through the ball and knees, but it certainly does not include the balance points at either the top of the spine or the elbow. Swing this way and your arms will move out of control while you try to rescue your balance.

CHECK THE HOLLOW

Another misconception you'll hear a Helpful Henry offer as advice is to keep your spine straight as you bend. The problem is that the spine is an S curve, and if it's set up correctly in balance the spine should form a hollow at the base of the back. Holding a shaft along your back helps verify that your spine is set up correctly as you bend forward from the hips.

Place the shaft of a club behind your back so that it touches you at both the base and top of the spine.

You should be able to slip your hand under the shaft into the hollow of your lower back if you set up correctly.

BODY TILT

Good posture at address also includes a body tilt to aid the turning of the backswing.

Tilt your spine 3 to 4 degrees away from the target. These drills help you understand how to set the correct body tilt. Your upper body needs to tilt slightly away from an up-and-down spine angle because the right hand placement is a little lower than the left on the club, and it helps you turn correctly on the backswing.

DRILLS

BALANCED POSTURE

CHIN TO LEFT LEG DRILL

1-CLUB ON CHIN

Begin by placing the clubhead at the base of your chin. The shaft should be supported so that it hangs down between the center of your stance.

2-BEND FROM THE HIPS

Keeping the club in the same position, bend forward from the hips to the correct balance position.

3-SET THE ANGLE

Maintaining the same forward bend and with the clubhead still touching your chin, shift your upper body until the butt of the club touches the inside of your left leg. This is the correct upper body tilt position.

BALANCED POSTURE

PUSH THE RIGHT HIP DRILL

1-INCORRECT SETUP POSITION

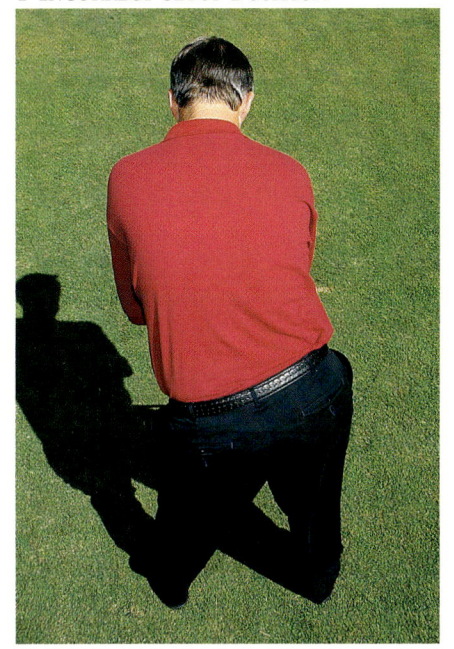

2-PUSH HIP SLIGHTLY

3-CORRECT TILT

Compare this common error photo with the two on the right. Some golfers push the right hip too high in the setup. The right hip drill corrects that problem.

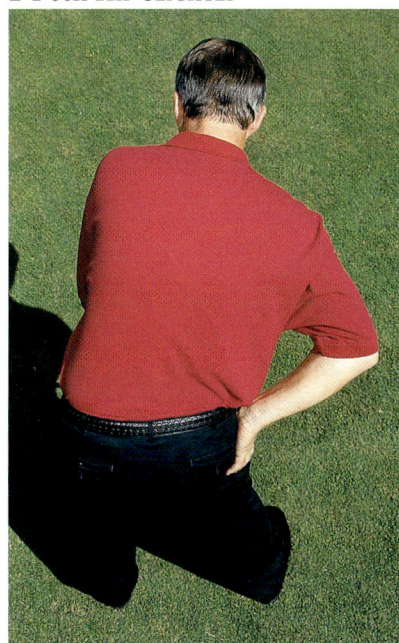

Place your right hand on your right hip and push it in slightly so that you begin to feel a little pressure on your left leg.

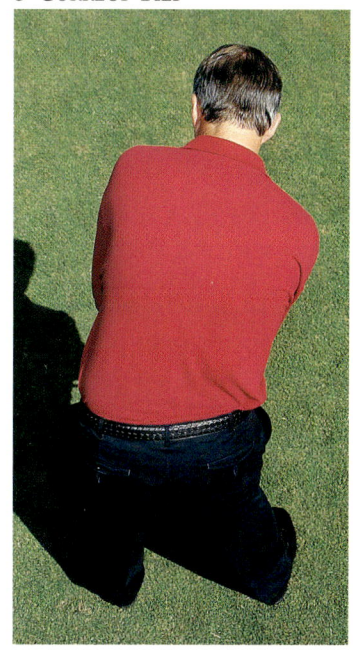

The upper body now has the correct tilt to help get your body into the correct position to move properly.

RIGHT SHOULDER TILT DRILL

Your right shoulder needs to be slightly lower in the setup than your left, because the right hand is lower than the left on the club. Poor takeaways and the falling domino problems that follow are attributable to the right shoulder getting too high or too level to the ground in the setup. This drill sets the correct shoulder tilt.

Cross your arms and hold a club across your level-to-the-ground shoulders (1). Tilting your right shoulder slightly down into the correct position is easy to verify by checking the shaft (2).

Building a Balanced Golf Swing

81

BALANCED HEAD

Head position is important to the balance of your golf swing. If your head gets tilted too much one way or the other, your balance is negatively affected because the fluid in your ears is sending out a rescue signal to the brain. When your eyes are level, the fluids in your ears are level.

Another misleading tip you sometimes hear suggests tilting your eyes left or right. Regardless of what direction you are tilting them, it has the adverse reaction of tilting your head. Keeping the ball in the center of your vision is a good safeguard against inadvertent head tilts.

Good athletes understand that keeping the ball in the center of their vision has a bearing on how solidly they hit the ball. Eyes update the brain on where things are, affecting the joints and how the muscles fire. Centering the ball in your vision and keeping your head level prevents an uncoordinated lunge to save the shot.

BALL CENTERED = LEVEL HEAD

BALL TO THE LEFT = HEAD TILTED TO THE RIGHT

BALL TO THE RIGHT = HEAD TILTED TO THE LEFT

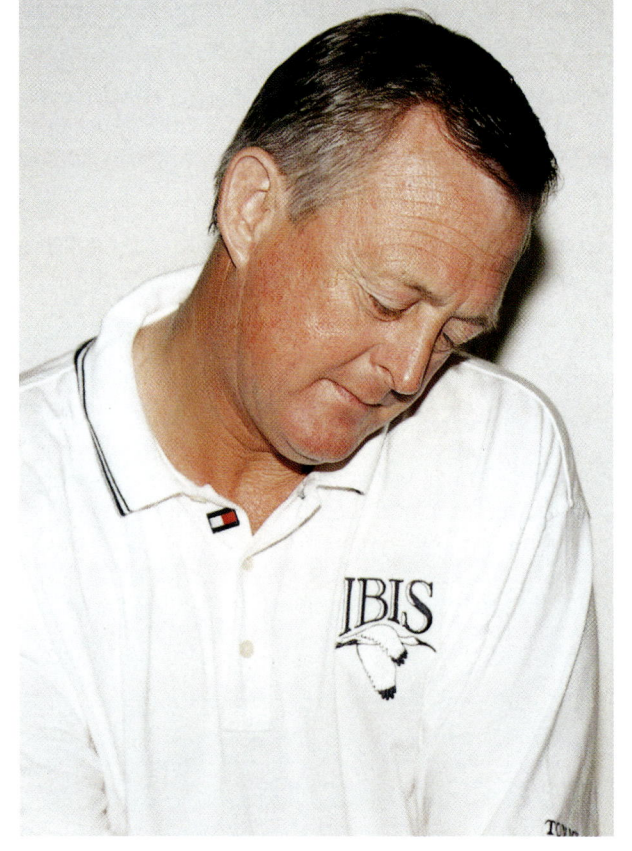

CHIN UP

Here's how to correct the *keep your head down* misconception that sticks your chin incorrectly into your chest.

CHIN UP = GOOD SHOULDER ROTATION

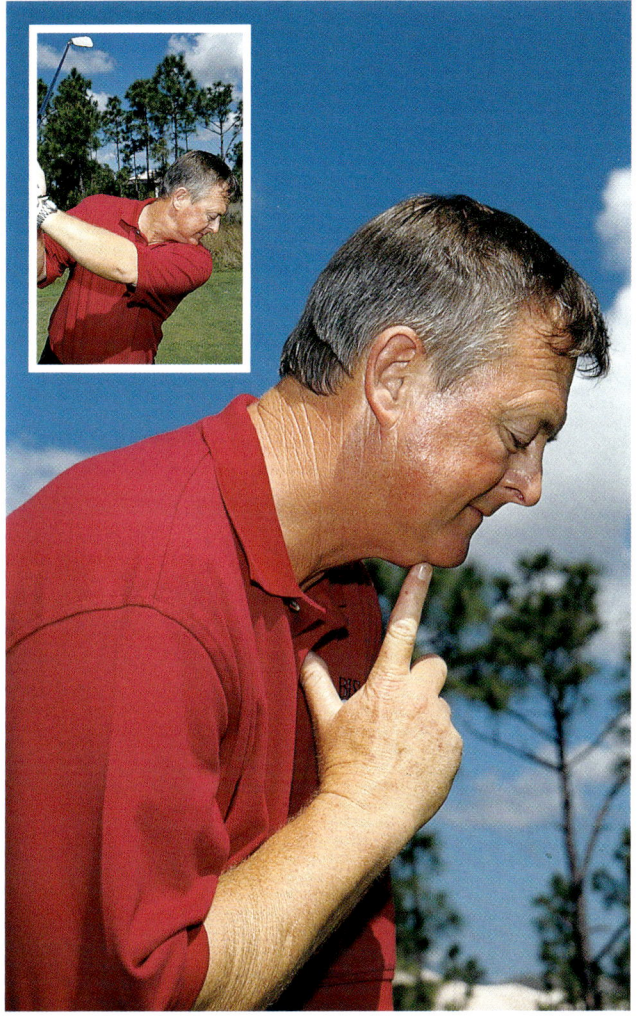

CHIN DOWN = SHOULDER-CHIN COLLISION

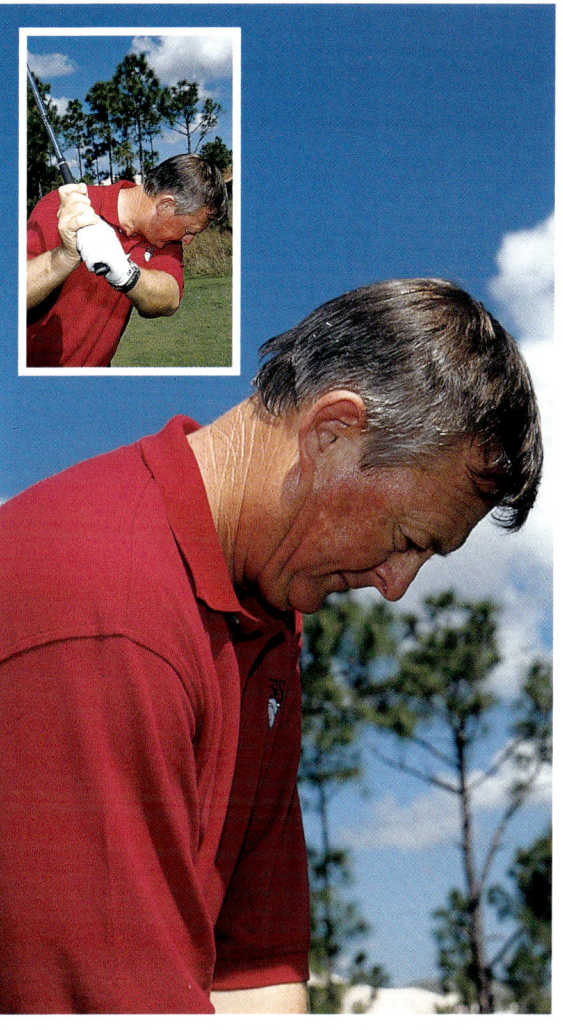

Placing your thumb on your chest and your extended index finger on your chin correctly places your chin up, allowing room for the shoulders to rotate under it during the backswing (inset).

Setting up with your head down leads to sticking your chin into your chest. Notice how the backswing collision with the turning shoulders (inset) knocks the club off the desired plane.

WEIGHT CHECK

Your weight should be on the middle of your feet. Some people say you need to be on your toes to be athletic, but that's not correct in golf. As you swing down into the ball there is a strong outward pull of the club, and you need something to resist that.

Weight on the middle of your feet acts as a counterbalance to the club's outward pull. If you make a mistake, it's better to err by having the weight more on your heels than on your toes.

GOOD ATHLETIC POSITION?

If you've heard a Helpful Henry-type say that you need to *set up in a good athletic position*, I have no idea what that means. We have either balanced our joints in line or we haven't. In my opinion golfers should think in terms of balancing their weight-bearing joints. This leads to balanced swings instead of becoming confused by *sound-good phrases* that mean absolutely nothing.

Dynamic Balance

You don't want your center of gravity wobbling around, because then your hands and arms, along with the club, will be all over the place. Maintaining a balance point while in motion constitutes dynamic balance.

Weight-bearing joints need to move in a way that allows the club to swing back and forth on a plane. Dynamic balance comes into effect because a certain amount of weight will be moving as you swing, and the balance points must move as well to remain balanced.

Martin retains his dynamic balance as the club is pulled down the swing plane into the power slot.

Balance occurs when you have equal amounts of weight on either side of a point. The trick to golf is that you are in motion while trying to keep your balance point. *Balance is more than just finishing your swing and holding the position. You must stay balanced as you are making the motion.*

TOUR players, like Scott McCarron shown earlier, are very balanced even when swinging at great clubhead speeds. Staying in dynamic balance ensures you do not get out of position while you're moving, giving yourself the best chance to smack the ball with the face square on the sweet spot.

Golfers also move body parts in opposing directions at the same time, taxing the ability to retain dynamic balance. The arrows in this example show that as the left shoulder and hip move closer to the ball, the right shoulder and hip are moving farther away from it.

DRILL

DYNAMIC BALANCE

THE BALANCE BEAM DRILL

Scott McCarron's Styrofoam log balance drill (page 78) is the advanced player version of this drill, and is the dessert to this serving of vegetables.

Like a gymnast, a golfer needs to keep his or her center of gravity over a particular point. You don't want to be too much on your toes or heels, or have your upper body tilted too far forward or too far back if you hope to stay on the beam. This drill helps develop the correct dynamic balance points throughout the golf swing.

Martin demonstrates how practicing on a 2x4 in your backyard helps develop dynamic balance.

1-SETUP

Begin doing this drill at home using only a tee but when you get to the practice range, tee up a ball to the height of the 2x4 and practice while hitting it. Start by putting yourself into the balanced posture position and shoulder tilt previously worked on.

2-BALANCED BACKSWING

Shifting the weight correctly into the backswing coil is a key dynamic balance position.

3-BALANCED DOWNSWING

Uncoiling the downswing shifts the dynamic balance point.

4-BALANCED IMPACT

As the club follows the correct swing plane toward impact, maintaining the dynamic balance is crucial to having a square-to-the-line clubface meet the center of the ball.

5-BALANCED FOLLOW-THROUGH

Finishing the swing in balance is another important dynamic balance position.

Building a Balanced Golf Swing

85

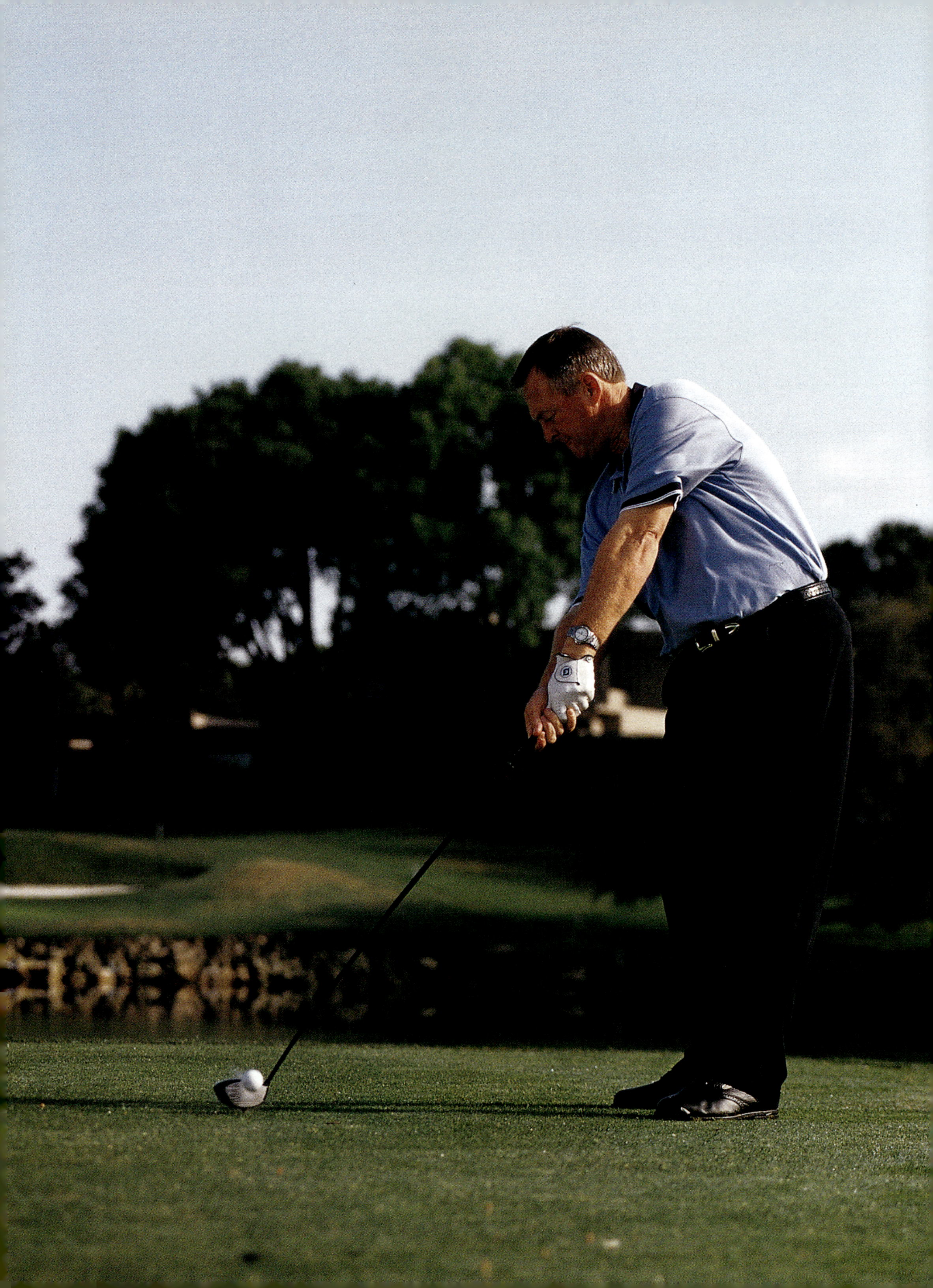

5 BACKSWING
ESTABLISHING GOLF'S BASIC GEOMETRY

Golf swings are similar to a train. You have a nice smooth ride when the engine is going at least as fast as the caboose. But if the caboose goes faster and tries to lead, the cars go off the track. In golf your hands are the caboose.
—Martin Hall

You might say I'm enjoying my dessert in the photo on the opposite page. The ball is leaving my driver's face, heading straight down the target line. In the only swing position that really counts, my clubface was square to the target line with the sweet spot smashing into the center of the ball at impact.

This shot was taken at 1/8000 of a second and even with of all my years of experience, both in teaching and playing, this was a moment I really had no conscious control over. What I did do, however, was capitalize on golf's basic geometry all through my golf swing to provide the best opportunity for accomplishing this excellent moment.

Building on the basic fundamentals learned and practiced in the last chapter, we can now begin building a repeatable, balanced, tilted-plane golf swing. You'll find the drills are fun to do while providing immediate feedback for nourishing your quickly growing understanding.

Train/Golf Synergy

Think of a train pulling the cars out of the station with the engine leading and the last car being the little red caboose. As a passenger in one of the cars you'll have a nice train ride as long as the train is going as fast as the trailing caboose.

If the caboose starts going faster than the engine, watch out for mayhem. Cars will be thrown off the track to the left and right, resulting in a major catastrophe.

Train	Golf
Engine	Feet, Knees and Hips
Train Cars	Arms
Caboose	Hands

Here's how the train and your golf swing components compare:

Even with a perfect setup, if your hands are going faster than your lower body, the club gets taken off the correct swing plane. Your goal is to get the correct geometry of the swing right and combine it with the correct order of motion in your takeaway, transition and downswing.

Martin's swing demonstrates excellent geometry along with proper tempo, timing and rhythm. Without the last three elements, his chances for squaring the clubface to the target line at impact would be diminished even though his swing positions are correct.

TEMPO, TIMING AND RHYTHM

It's a mistake to lump tempo, timing and rhythm into a single category, because they are not the same. *Tempo* is the speed of the swing and how long it takes to hit the ball. Some PGA TOUR players like Nick Price have a fast tempo compared to the slower tempo seen in Ernie Els's swing. *Timing* is the order of motion that comprises the golf swing. On the downswing the timing must begin from the ground up and work its way up the body. Rhythm is discussed below.

SWING DIRECTION	ORDER OF MOTION TIMING SEQUENCE
Backswing	1. Body 2. Arms 3. Wrists
Downswing	1. Feet 2. Knees 3. Hips 4. Shoulders 5. Arms 6. Wrists 7. Hands 8. Club

RHYTHM

Rhythm defines how we accelerate the club during the swing. I don't mind students being quick as they swing away from the ball … as long as they are quick going through it. The key is to balance that rhythm.

In the box below are some examples of good balanced rhythm and some examples of bad unbalanced rhythm. In the bad rhythm examples the caboose (hands) gets ahead of the engine (lower body).

Tempo, timing, rhythm and balance affect the face of the club. Analyzing a videotaped swing that looks good at all the positions the club goes through is one thing. But as good as the swing looks, if the rhythm were off, the clubface position would most likely not be correct at impact.

SWING CHECK	GOOD	GOOD	BAD	BAD
Takeaway	Quick	Slow	Slow	Quick
Top of Backswing	Slow	Slow	Slow	Slow
Transition	Slow	Slow	Quick	Quick
Downswing	Quick	Quick	Quick	Slow

Unbalanced rhythm has the ultimate effect of preventing the clubface from squaring up to the ball at the most important time in the swing: when the ball leaves the face at impact. Without proper rhythm, a clubface approaching the ball can either jolt open or snap shut too quickly.

You always see the great players like Phil Mickelson stand behind their ball—taking two or three purposeful practice swings, developing the rhythm of the motion. As you develop the correct geometry for your swing be aware of the need to also include tempo, timing, and rhythm into the whole package.

Drills

Backswing

Takeaway starts your clubhead moving away from the ball. Let's get right to the point by developing a good technique for making sure the club starts and follows the swing plane.

Martin's drills start the club back on the correct swing plane.

Windup Resistance Drill

The great players over the years, like Jack Nicklaus and Seve Ballesteros, have used versions of this drill to develop the feeling of winding up on the backswing against the resistance of the right leg. Nicklaus used a ball under his right foot, but Seve, whom I was able to watch when I competed against him, preferred using the grip of a club.

Setup

Begin by placing a club grip under the outside edge of your right foot.

Good

During the backswing coil, you should feel your weight on the inside edge of your right foot. Notice the foot is still in the same position as it was at setup.

Incorrect

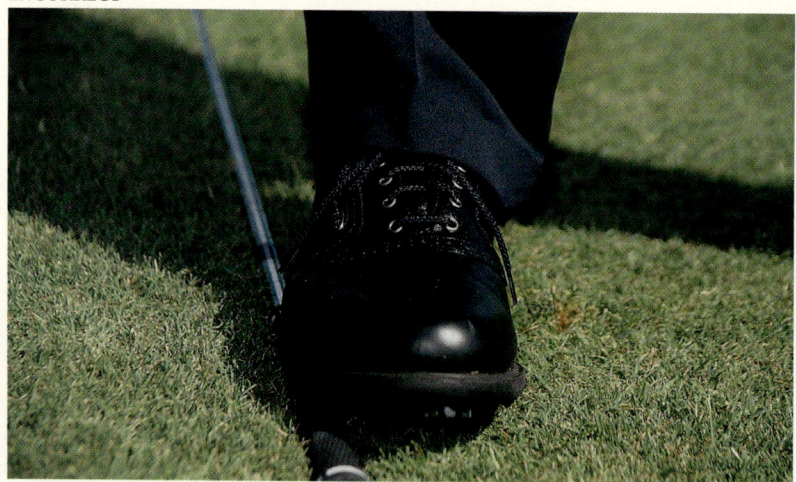

This is an example of incorrectly shifting the weight, which then wobbles the knee and leads to a rolling foot. Your foot should still be resting on the club during the backswing coil.

BACKSWING

TAKEAWAY DRILL

Practice your takeaway at home using two old shafts and a club on the ground to indicate the correct initial swing plane away from the ball.

GOOD TAKEAWAY

MISTAKE

Here's a great drill to get your club started away from the ball on plane. I'm using two old shafts, one painted blue on top and the other painted red. Position them so they are centered on the toe line represented by the club on the ground.

With the right foot touching the toe line shaft, the two painted clubs come into play on the backswing. The correct swing path away from the ball brings the shaft in contact with the closer pole, the red one in this example.

Touching the second pole (the blue one) is the most common mistake I see when someone lays the club off by twisting it in the wrong direction.

CROSSED SHAFT DRILL

This drill can also be practiced at home, where you can really spend some time building the correct swing. The crossed clubs serve as training aids for the correct backswing and follow-through shaft angle positions, in this case for the takeaway.

SETUP

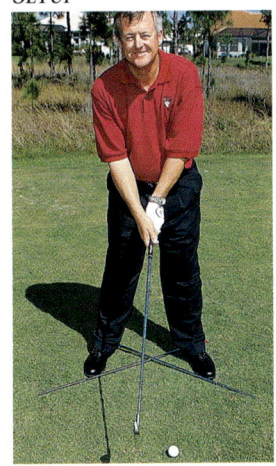

GOOD POSITION

MISTAKE

Take your stance and place one club so that it touches both your right heel and left toe. Place another club so that it touches both your left heel and right toe.

Check your shaft position on your takeaway. There should be a point in your takeaway where you can see that the club you are swinging is parallel to the shaft on the ground between your feet.

This photo represents an incorrect shaft angle position on takeaway. Continuing on with the backswing will take the club farther off plane. To correct this, slowly swing the club back repeatedly until the shaft appears to be parallel to the right-pointing shaft on the ground.

Backswing: Establishing Golf's Basic Geometry

BACKSWING

PRESET WRIST DRILL

Here's another drill I learned from Seve Ballesteros. It presets your wrists to make sure the left wrist cocks vertically on the backswing. This guards against laying the club off by preventing it from being twisted in the wrong direction.

1-SETUP

To begin, correctly set up to the ball and target line.

2-WRIST COCK

Cock the wrists vertically, raising the club straight up. Notice I have not lifted my arms but have only cocked my wrists. The club is now out in front of my body. Swing from this position.

3-SWING TO THE TOP OF YOUR BACKSWING

Continue by swinging the club back to the top of your backswing. This is a drill that can be done at home for developing the feeling, and then used at the practice range while hitting balls.

BACKSWING

TAKEAWAY ARM EXTENSION DRILL

The extension misconception was cleared up in Chapter 1. Understanding that your genetics determine the limit of your swing extension, this drill helps prevent you from allowing that natural extension to collapse on takeaway. **Caution: Do not hit balls while doing this drill.**

1-WHAT YOU NEED

Hobby shops or home improvement stores sell long wooden dowels and that's the only aid you'll need for this drill, along with a club.

2-SET THE NATURAL ARM EXTENSION

Set up to the ball, placing the dowel alongside the club shaft. Notice how the dowel acts as an extension reminder by lightly touching my body for the first part of the swing. The key is to be able to swing back while keeping the dowel in contact with your body. This drill should only be used for practice, not for hitting balls.

3-MAINTAIN TAKEAWAY ARM EXTENSION

Taking the club back while keeping the dowel touching the body maintains the natural arm extension set at address. You can't artificially extend your arms and hope to remain on plane, but this drill also stops the plane from collapsing by preventing the arms from coming too close to the body during takeaway.

Backswing: Establishing Golf's Basic Geometry

Backswing

Keep Hands Low Drill

Think about keeping your hands low in the takeaway, as opposed to keeping the club low (page 19). This is another drill that is for practice only but will help you feel where your hands should go.

1-Setup

For this drill I used several extra shafts and stuck them together but you can also use a broomstick or a long dowel. Notice how I set up the practice station by setting a club on the ground as a reminder of the target line. Next I inserted the shafts into the ground at about a 45-degree angle to act as a guide for my hands during the takeaway.

2-Address

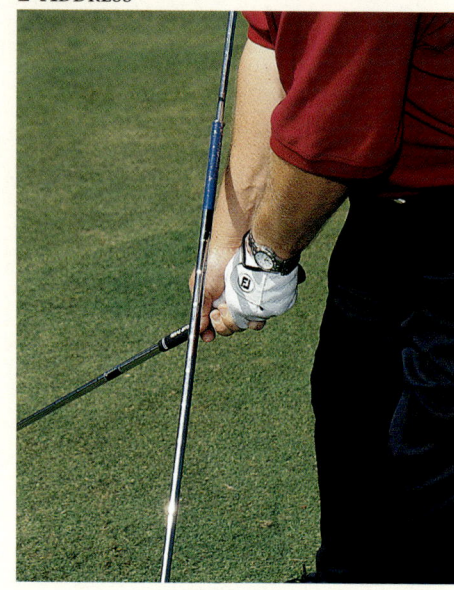

As you set up, copy my position at address: Keep your hands just underneath the tilted shaft.

3-Correct Swing Plane

As the club moves away from the ball, notice how my hands stay under the tilted shaft.

Mistake

The hands ran into the shafts as a result of laying off the shaft, which also twisted the clubface in the wrong direction.

BACKSWING

Takeaway Slot Drill

In this case I'm using the *All Pro Swing Trainer*, but you can build your own version by placing two shafts into the ground with two pieces of string attached in the same manner.

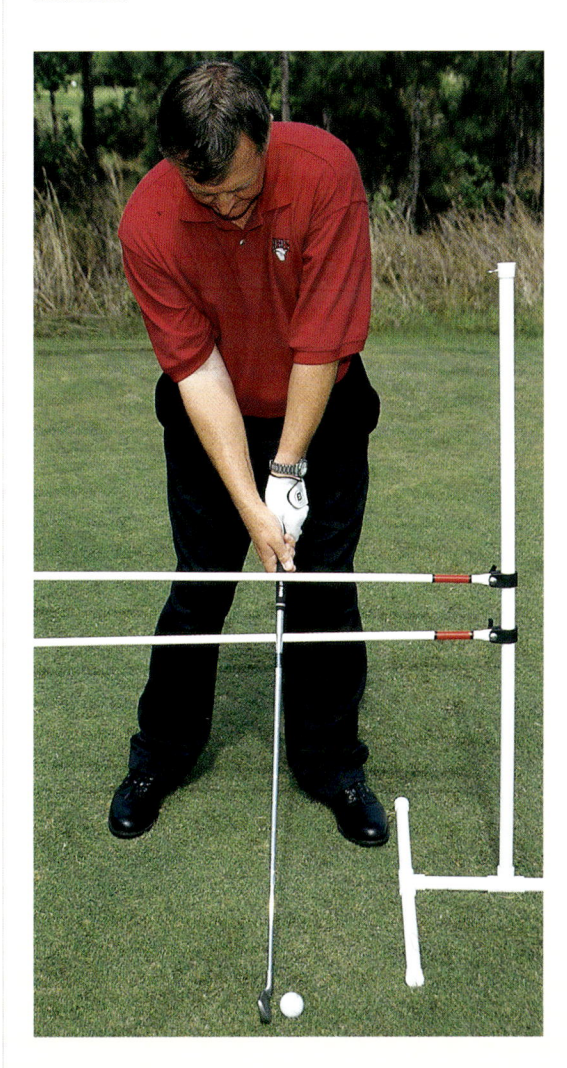

PERSONALIZED FEEL

All these drills are designed to help begin the golf swing on the correct swing plane. While I've included a wide selection and variety, and suggest you try them all, some drills may provide just the optimum personalized feeling you need to begin your swing correctly.

Instructors can talk all day about theory, but you will only develop the correct feeling by swinging several times with the drill or drills that help you learn where the plane really is.

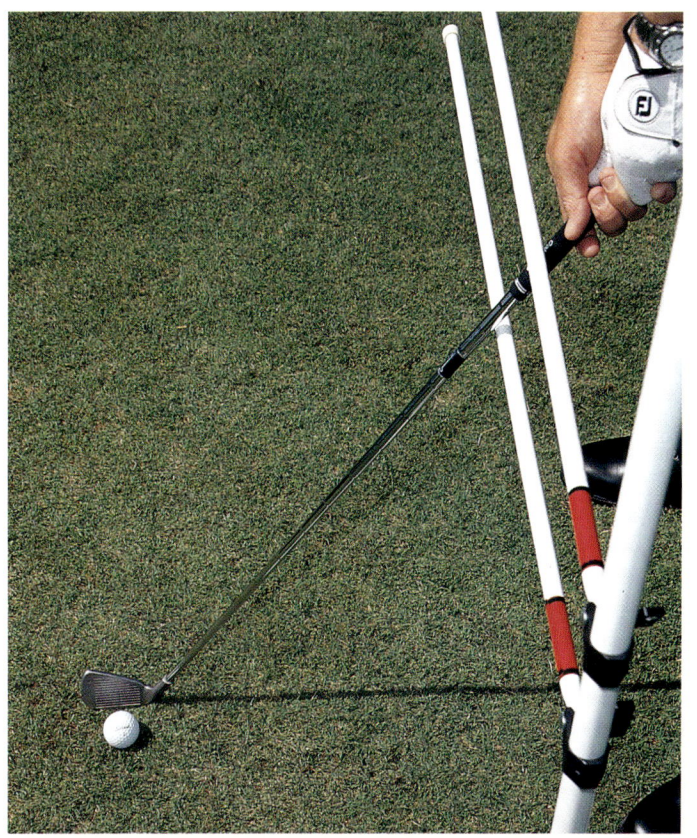

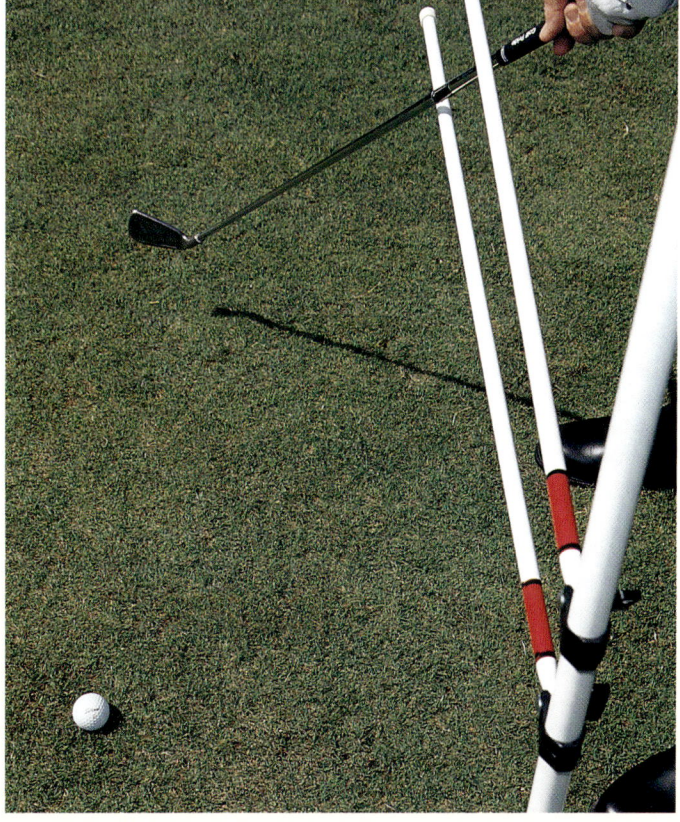

With the shaft placed between the two poles or string, swinging back gets the clubhead started along the correct swing plane.

Backswing: Establishing Golf's Basic Geometry

95

BACKSWING

CLUBFACE LOOKS AT BALL DRILL

To develop the correct takeaway swing plane, keep the eyes of the figure (drawn on the face of the club) looking at the ball for as long as possible. The one thing you *do not* want is to cause the face to look at the sky, instead of the ball, at any time during the takeaway.

Martin draws a face on his clubhead. The key to this drill is to keep the face of the club looking at the ball a little longer during the backswing.

ADDRESS

At the setup position, the face is looking directly at the ball.

A GOOD MENTAL IMAGE

As the club is swung away during the takeaway phase of the golf swing, notice how the face continues to look at the ball. Keep this image in mind to help you start the club back on the correct swing plane.

BACKSWING

LEFT ARM CHECK DRILL

To check for correct upper left arm position during takeaway, place a tee in your left armpit. It should not fall out until the backswing is well underway. The tee falling out too early in the takeaway warns you that the club will not be swung back on plane.

1-TEE IN LEFT ARMPIT

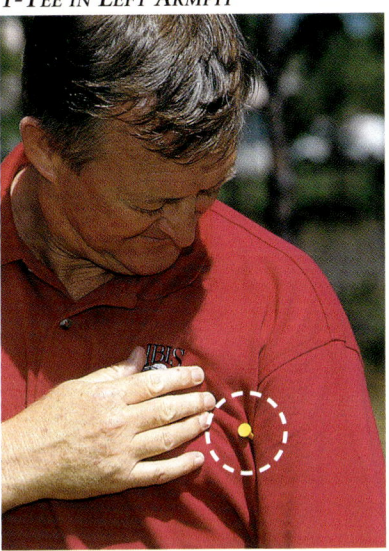

2-ADDRESS

Place the tee in your left armpit as a test to make sure the upper left arm remains close to the chest during the takeaway.

Address the ball with the tee inserted in your left armpit.

TAKEAWAY

GOOD POSITION

Notice the tee remains in place when the upper left arm stays close to the body during the takeaway.

It's okay for the tee to fall as the swing continues past takeaway. Keeping the upper left arm close to the body during the early stages of the swing helps start the club on the correct plane going back.

Backswing: Establishing Golf's Basic Geometry

DRILLS

BACKSWING COIL

Golf is a wind and unwind game, similar to throwing a discus in the way the body coils and uncoils its energy. Thinking in terms of weight shifting can be confusing and possibly inaccurate, so my suggestion is to reprogram your thought process to view your backswing as a coiling motion.

This series of drills show you how to coil your body up on the backswing correctly while still maintaining the correct swing path worked on earlier in the chapter.

TURN IN THE BARREL DRILL

Many of the PGA TOUR's top players have returned to the concept of swinging within a barrel, finding that it puts less pressure on their backs. Less pressure means fewer injuries. While taking some practice swings in your backyard or hitting balls on the practice range, pretend that you are standing in a barrel that comes up slightly above waist high as you swing to the top of your backswing.

Pretend you are standing in a barrel (1) while setting up to the ball. Take the club away from the ball following the correct swing path practiced earlier. Swing to the top of your backswing, keeping the club on the proper plane, coiling your lower body and trunk up so that you remain within the space of the imaginary barrel (2). Staying within the barrel shifts the weight properly as you coil up to the top of the backswing.

Pivot Drill #1

These two drills, working in conjunction with the barrel drill, help you make the correct coiling turn to the top of the backswing. The first drill develops lower body turn awareness. The second drill helps you program the correct feeling for a good backswing pivot.

1-Club Behind Thighs

2-Setup

3-Backswing Turn

To begin, place a ball on the ground and a club behind your thighs.

With the club being held behind your thighs and level to the ground, bend forward from the hips, placing yourself in a balanced setup position.

Keep the club level to the ground and, still pretending to be in a barrel, turn as if you were making a backswing, keeping the shaft touching both legs. Repeat slowly several times to develop the feeling of your lower body turning correctly.

Pivot Drill #2

1-Present the Tray

2-Serve to the Side

The second drill that helps develop the correct turn involves the visual image of serving a tray of drinks. From a balanced setup position, visualize you are holding a tray in front of you and slightly above waist high.

With your feet remaining flat on the ground and still maintaining the feeling of turning within the barrel, turn as if you were serving the tray to someone who had been standing alongside. Do this drill slowly and purposefully to program the correct feeling for the backswing pivot.

BACKSWING COIL

CROSSED CLUB PIVOT DRILL

This drill helps you develop the correct lower body pivot motion. At this point we are working on developing the correct backswing pivot, but this drill also provides a method for practicing your lower body motion throughout the swing.

BALANCED SETUP

Place two crossed clubs on the ground, positioning your feet in the open spaces, as I have. Bend forward from the hips into a balanced setup position. The shafts will guide the knees through the motion.

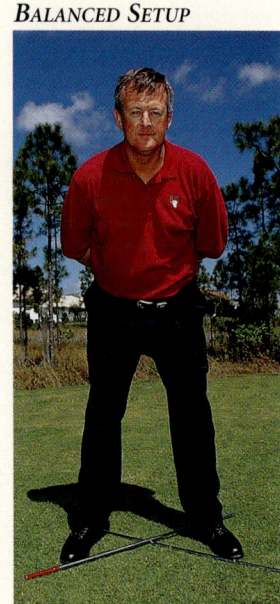

1-BACKSWING = LEFT KNEE TO RIGHT TOE

Turn your lower body with the feeling that your left knee is going toward your right toe following the left-heel/right-toe shaft.

2-DOWNSWING = RIGHT KNEE TO LEFT TOE

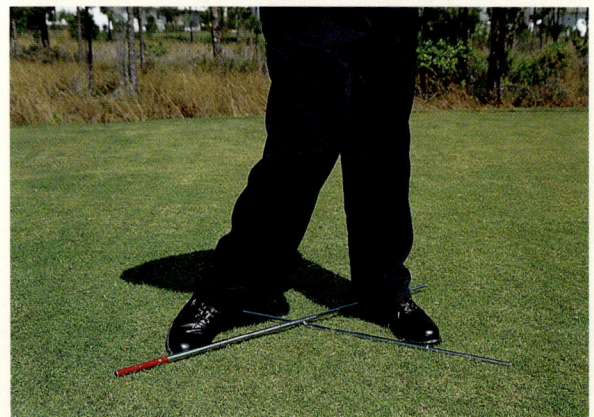

Practice your downswing turn by moving your right knee to your left toe following the right-heel/left-toe shaft.

REGULATE HIP TWIST DRILL

Many golfers have a problem with twisting their hips far too early in the takeaway. One of the best drills I know to stop this is to lift your right heel about one inch and swing to at least hip height before allowing your heel to return to the ground. This drill helps slow down the rate at which your hips are turning.

1-RAISE HEEL

From a balanced setup position raise your right heel about an inch (inset) prior to starting your backswing. This slows down your hip turn during takeaway.

2-RETURN HEEL TO GROUND

Once the shaft reaches the waist-high position, you can return your heel to the ground.

Golf Myths Exposed

100

BACKSWING COIL

NERF BALL DRILL

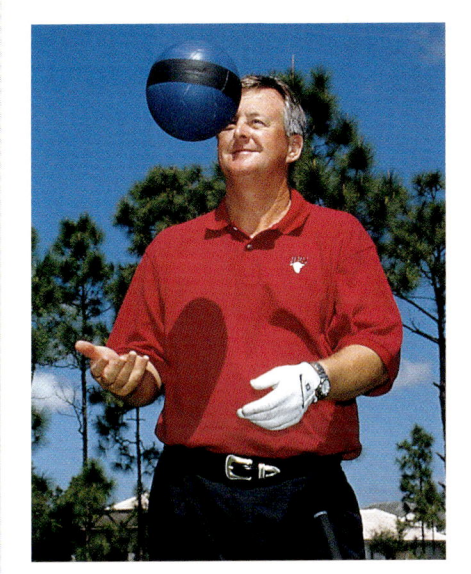

This drill eliminates the tendency to become a ballet dancer due to excessive leg motion during the backswing pivot. The key is to use a spongy ball that can be slightly compressed between your legs, like a smaller-than-regulation-size Nerf soccer ball. A beach ball would be too wide.

Martin uses a smaller-than-regulation-size Nerf soccer ball for this drill.

1-Place Between the Knees

I've put some tape on the ball to indicate the points for connecting my knees: I pinch the ball between my knees.

2-Backswing

Swing to the top of the backswing, barely squashing the ball with your knees. Make sure, however, that it remains in place as you go to the top of your backswing (inset).

3-Transition Release

The ball should only fall out as a result of your lower body motion toward the target as the transition from backswing to downswing begins.

Backswing: Establishing Golf's Basic Geometry

101

BACKSWING COIL

SHADOW COIL DRILL

Here's an excellent drill that immediately identifies a correct or incorrect backswing coil. This drill has two requirements:

1 - It must be a sunny day.

2 - The sun must be directly at your back so that your shadow is cast directly in front of you and not even slightly off to either side.

BALLS ON HIPS

CORRECT COIL

INCORRECT COIL

Place a ball on each edge of the shadow of your right and left hips. It's important the sun be directly behind you so the shadow can be cast directly in front of you.

As you swing back, coiling correctly, you should see a gap between the shadow of your left hip and that ball, but the right hip shadow does not go outside of the right ball. It's just as if you turned and coiled within the barrel, without touching its sides.

Both of these photos show examples of incorrect coiling on the backswing. In photo 1, the gap is incorrectly between the right ball and hip, and in photo 2, the right hip incorrectly passes the ball. This is the instant feedback you need to monitor the correctness of your backswing.

PRACTICE WITH A SHADOW

Tom Watson is a big believer in using the sun as a teaching tool. While some amateur players shy away or change angles so they are not bothered by their shadow, Watson will find a spot in the practice area to use the shadow in a positive manner for drills or as a check on his swing. Use the sun and your shadow to your advantage!

BACKSWING COIL

CONNECTION DRILL

Club President Tom Lehman stays connected.

PGA TOUR Partners Club President Tom Lehman maintains the connected relationship of his arms, hands and chest as he reaches the top of the backswing. Martin's drill develops your skills to stay connected when you reach the top, too.

SET UP THE DRILL

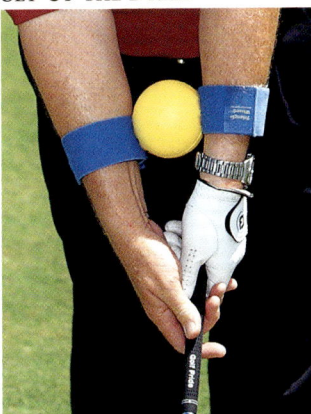

You can make some Velcro wrist cuffs and add some Velcro to a small ball, or you can contact Triangle Wizard Golf to purchase a training aid similar to the one I'm using. The key is to link your lower arms fairly close together with a small ball and then maintain this same relationship all the way through your golf swing.

CONNECTED BACKSWING

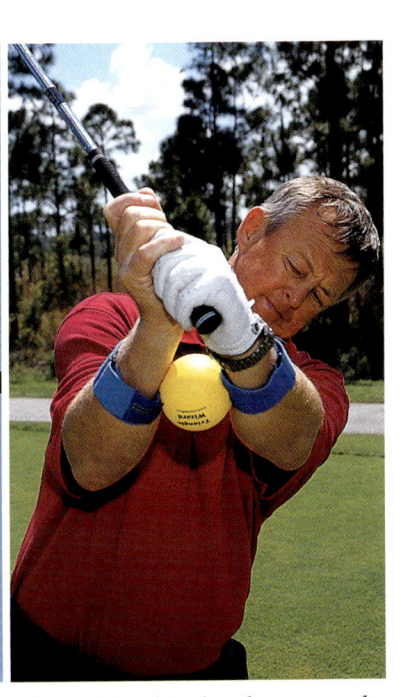

A connected backswing maintains the relationship of the hands, arms and chest that began at setup. This is verified during your swing because the wrists are still connected to the ball.

CONNECTION LOST

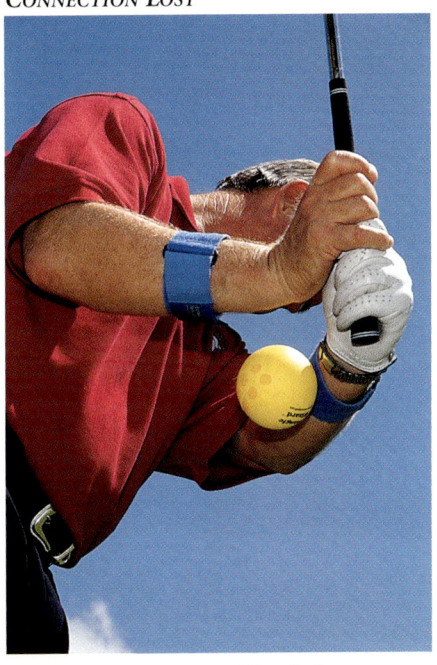

The wrists separate and break the connection with the ball in this incorrect backswing. This is the immediate feedback you need to improve, instead of wasting time practicing something incorrectly.

MARTIN SUGGESTS

I know there is a very successful training aid on the market that keeps your elbows linked during the swing, but I prefer that my students be able to tell immediately if their elbows are staying connected on their own.

The trouble with the elbow connector is that it forcibly keeps your elbows linked even if your arms are trying incorrectly to come apart. The type of aid seen in the photos here lets you see and hear immediately that your arms are trying to come apart. This immediate problem detection reveals that you must continue to work on this phase of your backswing until it's correct, instead of continuing to practice it incorrectly.

BACKSWING COIL

RIGHT WRIST BEND DRILL

To hit a very solid shot, your right wrist needs to be bent at impact. The best way to accomplish this is to make sure your wrist is bent as it reaches the top of the backswing. If the wrist is vertical instead of bent at the top, it's almost impossible to create the bend on the way down to the ball. To create the correct bend, practice balancing a tray in your right hand at the top of your backswing.

Martin demonstrates the amount of right wrist bend needed at both the top of the backswing and at impact. If you slice the ball, this is a very good drill to change that slice into a draw.

Supporting a tray in your right hand at the top of the backswing sets the correct angle for your right wrist (1). Practice the backswing from the address position, swinging the tray up to the top with your right hand and the club in your left (2) to develop the correct, consistent wrist bend.

RIGHT ELBOW IN FRONT OF THE BODY DRILL

This is another excellent drill to develop the correct technique for keeping your elbows linked properly.

1-Set Up

2-Raise Club

Maintain the same position and raise the club up vertically in front.

3-Make Backswing

To set up, hold the club in your right hand. Place your left hand behind your right elbow. The left hand acts as a governor to keep the right elbow in front of the body during the backswing.

Swing back to the top of your backswing. The left hand behind the right elbow prevents it from moving independently out of the correct position.

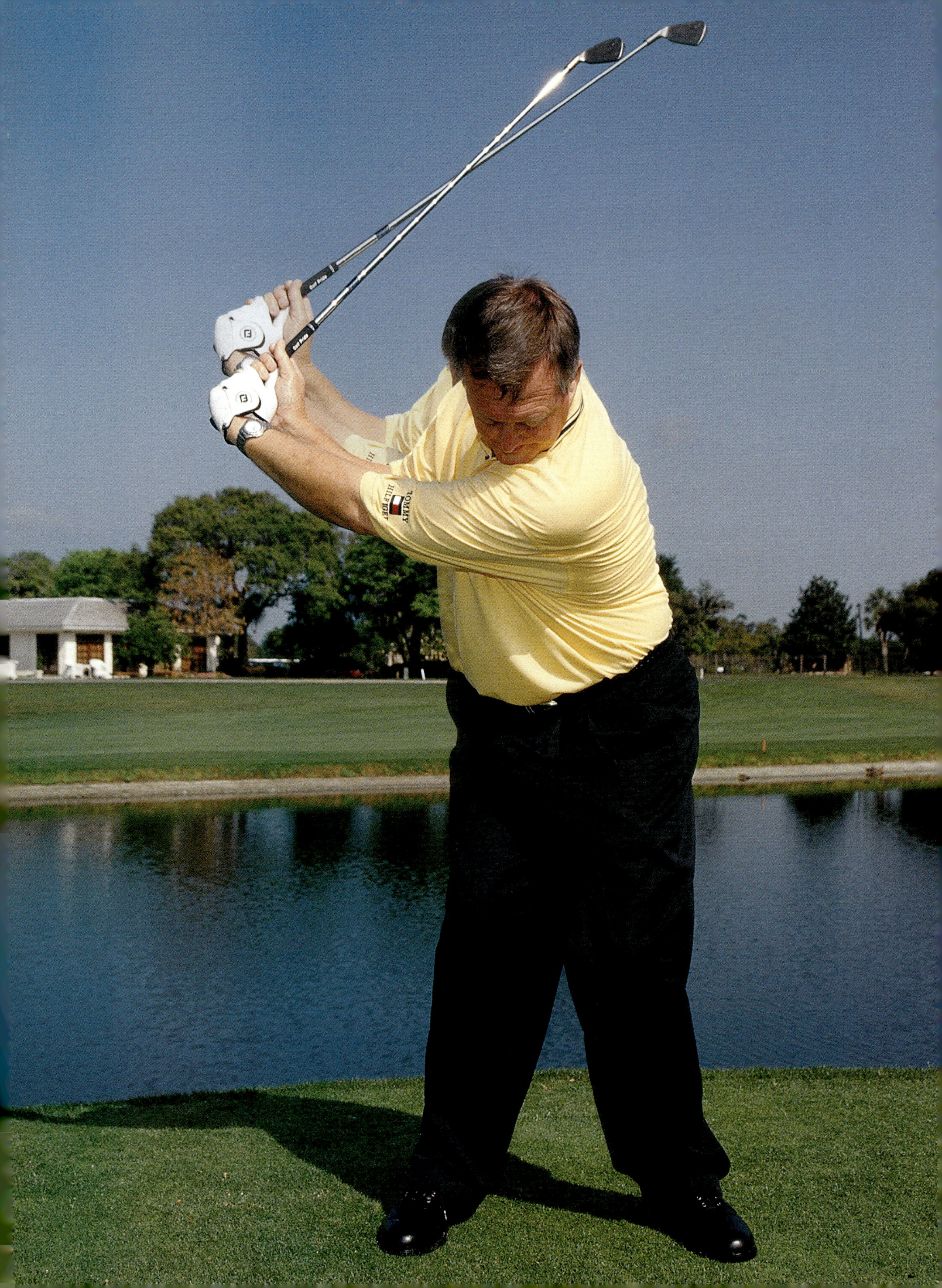

6 TRANSITION

Your transition needs to be balanced and steady. You don't want an earthquake going on at command center when you're trying to run an operation. —Martin Hall

Transition is where the end of the backswing blends with the start of the downswing. This is the crossroads where some golfers really head down the wrong path to a virtual train wreck.

Following the correct sequence of motion maintains the balance needed throughout the swing, keeping the clubhead on the correct swing plane. Over-acceleration is the enemy! Smooth acceleration brings the clubhead to the ball with maximum power.

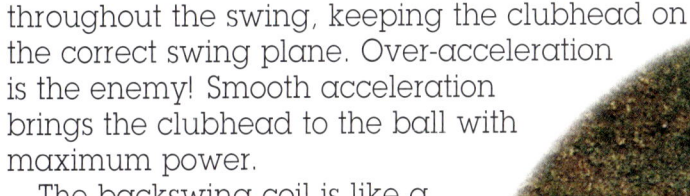

The backswing coil is like a powerful spring waiting to be released, and how you transition into the downswing, correctly releasing that stored up energy, is covered in this chapter. The drills will keep you on the correct plane to smack the back of the ball with a square face at impact.

The Balanced Transition

Your lower body begins the transition from the backswing to the downswing. With a square-to-the-target-line clubface at impact being the ultimate goal, the club must start down a very specific geometrical swing arc, as the next two sets of photos show.

Transition: Face-On View

The transition does not release the energy coiled up during the backswing, as the shirt wrinkles wrapped around my torso clearly show. It only begins the process of smoothly shifting from reverse to forward. The club position has moved only from the lower body's initial shift and rotation toward the target. My shoulders and arms have not yet begun their return, and I remain powerfully coiled.

Transition from the Front

The circle around my belt buckle in both photos shows the hip rotation has begun in photo 1. The keys to a good transition can best be seen in the positions of the left knee (arrow) and left hip in photo 2. Both have started to shift toward the target.

Transition: View from Above

From this position, the clubhead can follow the correct swing path to the ball. If I were to make the mistake of overaccelerating with the hands, wrists and arms, power would be lost, not retained, and the clubface might be forced off the correct tilted-oval swing plane. The correct, orderly clubface rotation would be negatively affected and the face would not impact the ball square to the target line.

Transition from Above

As seen from above, the initial shifting of my lower body toward the target from the top of the backswing (1) to the downswing (2) has maintained the connection of the chest, arms and hands. The flexing club shaft indicates that the power stored up during the backswing coil is now on the verge of being released to the ball.

Pick the More Powerful Position

The choice is simple. Photo 1 shows the correct transition, featuring only the lower body motion beginning. The upper body torso is still powerfully wound up and ready to be released.

Photo 2 shows the common mistake of a shoulder and arm transition. No lower body motion has begun. Power, as well as accuracy, has been squandered. The drills will have your transition looking like photo 1.

Transition

DRILLS

TRANSITION

LEFT HAND OVER LAP DRILL

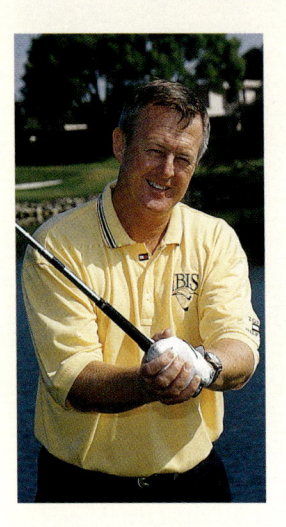

Some transition problems are the result of wanting your right hand to do it all. This drill stops the right hand, right wrist and right arm from thrusting and lashing during the direction change from backswing to downswing.

The hit impulse will be reduced by doing this drill with the drill on page 111. Both drills keep everything connected and the clubhead correctly lagging behind in the correct sequence. The engine stays ahead of the caboose.

ENGINE AND CABOOSE

Just like a train, your golf swing will be fine as long as it stays on the correct track. Your body is the engine, the arms are the cars and the hands are the caboose. Everything is fine with the train and your swing as long as the engine is going as fast as the caboose.

But if the caboose, or in this case your hands, go faster than your body, the train and your swing will derail from their respective tracks. These drills will help you master the correct order of motion and timing.

1-RIGHT OVER LEFT

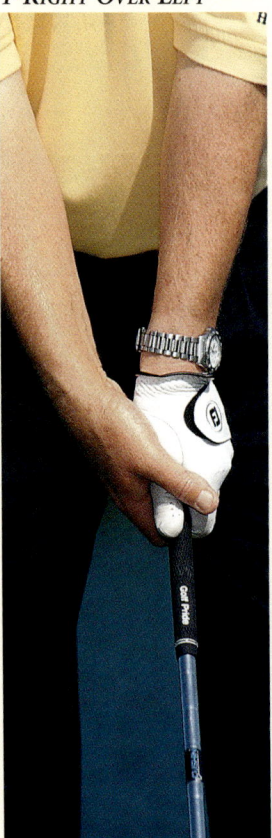

2-LOWER BODY DOES THE PULLING

To begin the drill, overlap the right hand on top of the left instead of setting up with your normal grip.

With your right hand over your left, coil up into the correct backswing position (1). Feel how everything stays together. Without starting any shoulder or arm rotational movements toward the ball, allow the transition to begin with the lower body. Start from the ground up. The connected feeling comes as the lower body pulls the shoulders, arms and hands into the downswing (2).

TRANSITION

SWING AND LET GO DRILL

1-RIGHT HAND OVER LEFT DOWNSWING

This is the second drill you need to stop your right hand, wrist and arm from *the hit impulse* to do it all.

Continue the downswing with the right hand still overlapping the left.

2-LET GO

Just as you get into the hitting area, allow the right hand to slip off the left (1). Only the left arm and hand will take the club through to finish (2).

TRANSITION

STEP-IN DRILL

This sequence drill makes sure your engine stays in front of your caboose, keeping your golf swing on the correct track. That's the transition theme: The engine must go at least as fast as the caboose.

This drill makes sure the downswing unwinds from the ground up in this order:

1 - Feet

2 - Knees

3 - Hips

4 - Shoulder

5 - Arms

6 - Hands

7 - Clubhead

As you first try this drill, the initial tendency is to swing the club down before taking the step, which is a good indication that you've been over-accelerating your hands at the start of the transition. This drill eliminates that problem and trains you to follow the correct sequence of motion.

1-SET UP BEHIND

Take your normal setup with the clubface behind the ball. Then put your left foot beside your right foot and then the clubhead in front of the feet.

2-BACKSWING

With your feet together, coil to the top of the backswing.

3-STEP FORWARD

Maintain the same upper body position and step into the position your left foot would normally occupy.

4-STEP FIRST/SWING SECOND

Begin your balanced transition from the ground up without allowing your shoulders and arms to swing at the ball. If you have a problem swinging down before stepping in, you've been trying to overaccelerate your hands from the top instead of beginning the transition from the ground up.

DRILLS

SMOOTH ACCELERATION

The three drills here ensure that your arms gently accelerate from the top. The key is to let your body get into a correct position before the force goes out to the head of the club.

This smooth acceleration is like going through the gears of a well-tuned sports car. You wouldn't start out in fifth gear or it would jerk, sputter and probably stall. Smooth acceleration develops maximum clubhead velocity along with a square-to-the-target-line clubface position meeting the golf ball at impact.

SMOOTH ACCELERATION DRILL #1: DROP THE BALL

Transitions that begin from the ground work their way up to the left knee, which begins the return toward the target. When the sequence of motion is correct, a slight bowing of the left knee will release a ball placed between the knees at setup. **The goal: The training ball (see below) must hit the ground before your club hits the golf ball.**

1-BALL BETWEEN LEGS

Place a soft, but not too large, ball between your knees. This training ball should stay in place until your legs enter the transition movement back to the target.

2-COILED BACKSWING

The ball remains in place to the top of the backswing.

3-LOWER BODY TRANSITION

The ball will drop to the ground when transition begins from the ground up. Notice how my left knee leads the way back toward the target, and in doing so creates a gap that allows the ball to fall. The correct sequence has begun.

THE HELPFUL BALL

Do not use a beach ball for the *drop the ball drill*. It's too big! There must be some foot and knee motion to both the backswing and downswing, and larger training balls will hinder that motion. Instead, find a medium-sized Nerf-type ball that has some elasticity to it. You don't want to crush it with your legs, only exert enough pressure to pin it between your knees on the backswing and have it drop as the left knee begins its move toward the target.

Transition

Smooth Acceleration Drill #2: Maintain the Tension

This is one of my favorite drills because of its immediate graphic feedback for transitioning correctly or incorrectly. The key is to maintain the same tension in the tubing at transition as was present at the top of the backswing.

A lower body transition accomplishes that goal, and the tubing stays tight and full of energy. But an incorrect shoulder- and arm-led transition eliminates the tension and built-up energy, causing the tubing to immediately and graphically slacken.

Martin is using a piece of surgical tubing for this drill, but you can also use a rope. Just take up the slack at the top of the swing.

1-Tie the Tubing

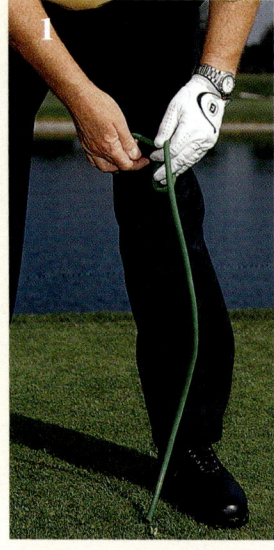

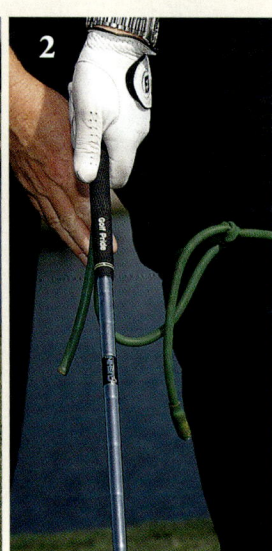

I'm using surgical tubing but you can also use a piece of rope. Begin by tying the tubing to the left thigh (1) and hold the other end under your hands when gripping the club (2).

2-Set the Tension

Coiling into the correct backswing position will take all the slack out as the tubing stretches. If you use rope, take the slack out at this position by pulling the string up into the grip.

3-No Slack = Correct Transition

The tension in the line is retained as the lower body correctly leads the way.

4-Slack = Incorrect Transition

If you incorrectly start the transition from backswing to downswing with your shoulders and arms, the line will slacken immediately. Repeatedly practice this drill at home to program your muscle memory correctly.

SMOOTH ACCELERATION DRILL #3: RELATIONSHIP DRILL

MAINTAIN THE DISTANCE

In your mind's eye, don't think of swinging the head of the club from the top. Instead, think that your shaft needs to maintain the same distance from the shoulder during the initial portion of the downswing ... a smooth sweep.

This industrial-strength version of the tension drill offers a good visual presentation of just exactly that. It may be easier viewed than done while building the correct mental image of what the sequence of motion needs to be in a correct transition.

Using this device, I begin by coiling to the top of my backswing. Notice the bend is attached to the shaft and touching my shoulder (1). During the transition led by the lower body, the two remain in contact (2 and 3). This keeps the caboose behind the engine with a downswing sequence where the club lags behind the lower body through impact.

Transition

115

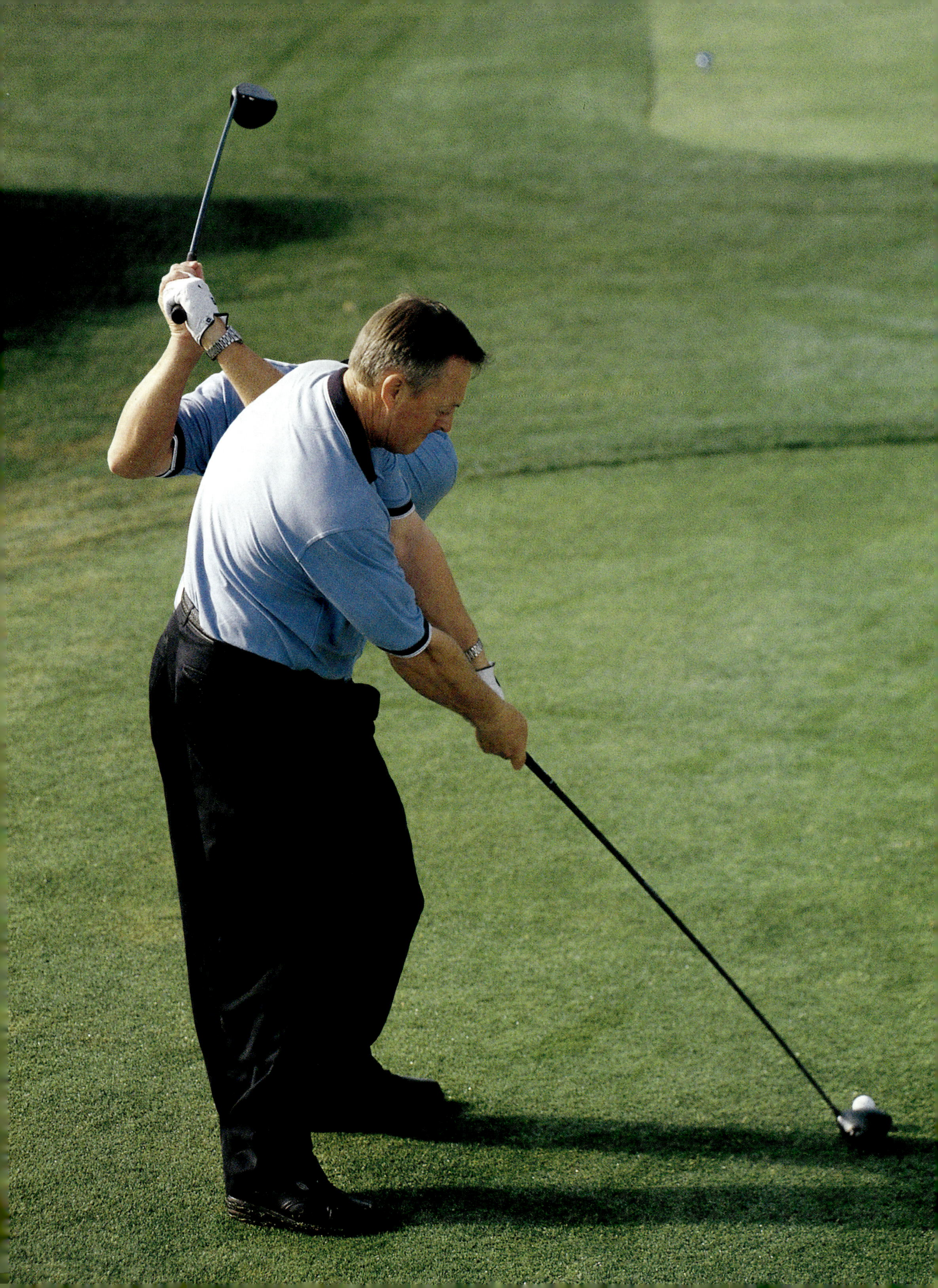

7 Downswing to Impact

The more your center of gravity stays steady, the less complicated the task of getting your clubhead to meet the ball correctly. —Martin Hall

Swinging the club toward the target and having the ball leave a square-to-the-target-line clubface at impact is the ultimate goal of the golf swing. But equally important is being able to compress the ball with a solid hit. Your hands should be ahead of the ball at impact to deliver this power punch.

A myth that many golfers believe is that swing speed is totally responsible for distance. Consequently, their swings suffer by counterproductive efforts to make the clubhead go faster. The distances that balls travel are not attributable to clubhead speed alone. Speed, by itself, is not power! Mass is part of the equation, too, and it's enhanced by having the hands slightly ahead of the ball at impact: the caboose staying behind the engine.

Solid, accurate hits are the goal, and the drills in this chapter will keep your clubhead on the right path to the ball. Following this solid path to progress and improvement means you'll never be suckered by quick-fix swing misconceptions again.

Goal: Solid Hits

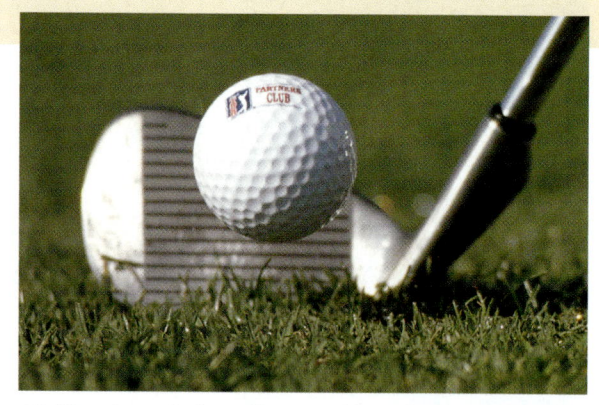

If you're driving along the turnpike at 70 mph and a bug hits your windshield, the windshield will not be damaged. But if you're driving at 50 mph and a pebble hits your windshield, it will chip. If a brick hits your windshield when you're traveling at 30 mph, it will go right through it.

Mass makes the difference in force, and is an important factor (along with clubhead speed) in ultimately determining how far a ball can go.

When your hands are slightly ahead at impact, mass becomes a factor in the swing. But if your hands are even fractionally behind the ball, there is no mass, and the effect is the same as the bug going into a windshield.

Clubhead speed alone does not determine how far a ball can go. Compressing it at impact, as a result of following the correct plane with the hands being slightly ahead, creates the mass factor.

Iron vs. Driver Shaft Angles

At impact, better players' driver shaft angles will differ from their iron shaft angles. Ideally, the driver shaft should be almost vertical at impact, while an iron shaft should have a target-forward lean angle of between 8 and 10 degrees.

That's one of the reasons the PGA TOUR professionals never look like they are thrashing at the ball, but less skilled players do. The lean of a pro's shaft at impact (as a result of following the correct order of motion, which allows the clubhead to rotate properly while following the swing plane) places the hands slightly ahead of the ball. This develops mass and a solid hit.

Martin's hands are slightly ahead as his clubhead is about to strike the ball.

SENIOR PGA TOUR professional John Jacobs frequently leads The SENIOR TOUR in driving distance. Notice, at this moment of impact, how his hands are slightly ahead of the tee as the ball leaves the clubface.

Martin's Key to Power Golf

One of the keys to power golf is to visualize yourself in a swimming pool. As you swing down to the ball, at least one knuckle of your left hand has to get into the water before the clubhead does. If the clubhead gets into the water first, you will lose all the power in the swing.

Golf Myths Exposed

HIT IMPULSE: A ROGUES' GALLERY

Here are some of the worst things that can happen during the downswing to impact position. We call it a rogues' gallery of things you don't want to be doing during your golf swing.

GOOD FOOTWORK

EXCESSIVE FOOTWORK

Raising your heels takes stability out of the swing and makes you want to hit that ball now. This produces a burning desire to administer brute force and get the swing over with, leading some golfers to raise either their left or right heels during the downswing.

Good players plant themselves firmly on the ground at impact, with the exception of the really long hitters who are sometimes pushing so hard into the ground with their feet that centrifugal force lifts their heels slightly off the ground; that is not something you should copy.

LEFT WRIST COLLAPSE

Collapsed   **Good**

You simply cannot have power if the shaft is past your left arm at impact (large photo). It's just not possible. Instincts incorrectly tell you to get the clubhead to the ball when you really should be trying to drag the whole shaft through instead (inset).

BENDING ELBOWS

Bad   **Good**

Pulling your hands into your body causes this bending elbow problem (larger photo). The problem occurs because it's physically demanding to keep the elbows together during the golf swing, and it's a lot easier to pull the hands in because the shoulders don't have to turn as much.

The inset photo shows how the arms should be extended at impact to deliver all the energy produced in the swing to the ball.

Downswing to Impact

Drills

Impact

The only part of the golf swing that really matters is impact. Unfortunately, it's also the one part of the swing you are least able to control, because the club is going its fastest at that moment.

It's sort of the Zen side of golf. As an instructor I can say, "I want your impact to be correct, and by the way, don't try to control your impact because you can't!"

What you can do, however, are these drills. You'll find that *trapping the ball* gives you the correct impact feeling. Once you are pretty correct two or three feet prior to reaching the ball and correct two or three feet after hitting the ball, then the impact should be fairly good.

The ball's flight will give you the best idea of what to adjust to improve your impact. For instance, if the ball continues fading or slicing to the right, you need to do something to close the clubface. If the ball hooks or draws too much to the left, you need to do something to keep the clubface from closing so quickly. If the ball flight is too high, your change has to involve de-lofting the club, and if ball flight is too low, you need to make a change that adds loft.

Gardner Dickinson Drill

This drill, named after a great player and teacher, gives you the strength in the "hit" part of the formula. By placing yourself in the perfect impact position, the drill takes the club back to hip height and returns it to impact three times before hitting a solid shot.

1-Balanced Setup

2-Impact Position

3-Hip-High Backswing

Address the ball with the correct grip and a balanced posture. Always make sure the ball is positioned in your stance correctly anytime you use a ball in the drills.

Without hitting the ball, put yourself in the ideal impact position with your hands ahead of the ball.

Without moving your legs, swing the club back so the shaft reaches a hip-high and parallel-to-the-ground position. Check to make sure the shaft is also parallel to the target line.

4-Return to Impact

5-Repeat Without Hitting

Without hitting the ball, return the clubhead to the impact position.

Repeat this step one more time without hitting the ball, making sure your impact position has the hands ahead.

6-Repeat and Hit

1

2

The third time after taking the club back from the impact position (1) to the hip-high level, hit the ball (2) on the downswing. Finish at about waist level.

This drill's swing symmetry should be from waist high on the backswing to waist high on the follow-through.

See if you make solid contact and hit a straight shot. If you don't, then keep doing the drill until you can. This gets back to the vegetables before dessert idea. Half swings must be mastered before full swings can be properly done.

Look at the Nail

As you work on the Gardner Dickinson drill, think in terms of how you hammer a nail. Look at the inside back of the ball just as you would look at the head of a nail you're about to strike. This sharpens your senses to get the sweet spot of the club to smash up against the *back inside quadrant* of the ball.

Downswing to Impact

IMPACT

COMPRESSION DRILL

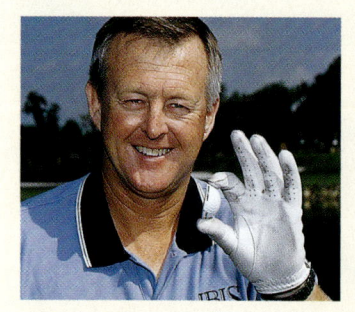

Martin uses only half a ball for this drill.

This drill ingrains into your subconscious what it's like to give the ball a downward hit. Probably not one golfer in 10 has an angle of attack that hits down on the ball with their irons.

This helps to get the low point of the swing arc beyond the golf ball, creating post-impact divots. I cut a ball in half, but you can also stand on a range ball pushing it halfway into the ground. You won't be hitting the ball.

1-Setup

Place a tee about two inches ahead, on the target side of the ball, but set up in a balanced posture position that addresses the half ball (inset).

2-Hit the Tee

From a short backswing, swing down with the goal of hitting the tee but missing the ball.

3-Miss the Ball/Hit the Tee

The purpose for using the half ball (or buried ball) is so the club will just pass over it on the downswing but still hit the tee two inches in front. The drill helps you slightly extend the bottom of your swing arc nearer to the target and beyond its normal position.

After repeating this drill two or three times, use the same short backswing and hit a real ball that is not pushed into the ground. The ball flight will probably be lower than normal, but your contact will be "squeezed" because the ball will be trapped against the ground. It also helps hand-eye coordination. Gradually lengthen this drill to a three-quarter swing and then to a full swing.

IMPACT

FOOT POLICE DRILL

This is a Jack Nicklaus drill I learned from his longtime instructor Jack Grout. Grout wanted young Jack to learn how to hit shots while rolling on the insteps—the left instep going back and the right instep going through. Placing a shaft over the right ankle prevents the heel from rising.

CALL THE FOOT POLICE

This drill will stop the problem of raising the right heel (circle) during the swing.

1-FOOT ANCHOR

Place a shaft over your right ankle to act as a foot policeman to stop your heel from rising during the swing.

2-ROLL INSTEAD OF LIFT

On the downswing, practice by first rolling onto the instep of your right foot before hitting the ball. This helps keep you down and "in the shot" so the force goes into the ball.

"PICTURE THIS" DRILL

Placing some shafts around my body with bungie cords shows the correct impact positions for the hips and shoulders.

- A line across the shoulders should be parallel to the intended flight line.

- A line across your hips should be pointing to the left of the intended flight. This is also referred to as being open.

Martin demonstrates shoulder and hip positions at impact.

Downswing to Impact

IMPACT

ENERGY TRANSFER DRILL

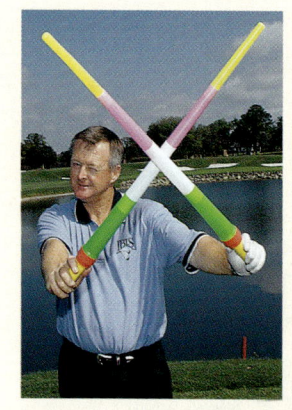

1-Downswing

Martin uses some collapsible toy swords for demonstrating the swing point where energy needs to be transferred through the clubhead to the ball for power.

The swords stay collapsed, as they should, during this phase of the downswing because it's premature to transfer the energy to the clubhead.

2-Bottom of the Arc = Energy Transferred

3-Squandered Energy

A powerful golf swing transfers the energy down through the clubhead at the bottom of the swing arc. And what little white object is supposed to be there? The ball, of course!

If the energy is released too early, power is lost. Rummaging through a toy store, I came across the ideal props to dramatically illustrate this, and developed a drill using them.

Do you remember the old collapsible toy swords some of us played with as kids? They are making them again and I suggest purchasing a pair to help develop a powerful impact.

The swords extend out, dramatically demonstrating the energy being transferred through them. In the golf swing, energy is transferred through the clubhead to the ball at this same point—the point of impact!

Energy was transferred out to the swords too early in this incorrect downswing. This same early transfer during the golf swing produces weak, inaccurate shots.

IMPACT

GENTLE ELBOW PUSH DRILL

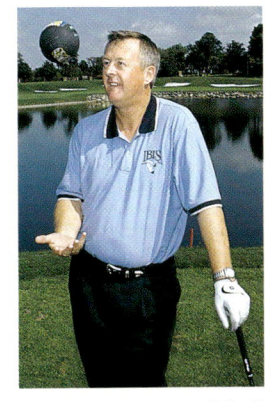

Through the swing there should be a very gentle pushing together of the elbows. This doesn't mean they are rigid, but there is some gentle pushing inward with just enough pressure to prevent them from coming apart.

All the great players and teachers throughout the years, like Ben Hogan and Harvey Penick, felt what a great thought it is to keep the elbows the same distance apart during the entire golf swing.

I use a ball for my drills because the training aid straps sold in golf stores artificially lock the position in but do not let you know if the elbows still want to come apart. By keeping the ball in place during the swing, you know instantly that you are improving. *You* have to do the training, not the straps.

Martin uses a small ball to help train the elbows to stay in position during the downswing-to-impact positions.

BALL BETWEEN WRISTS

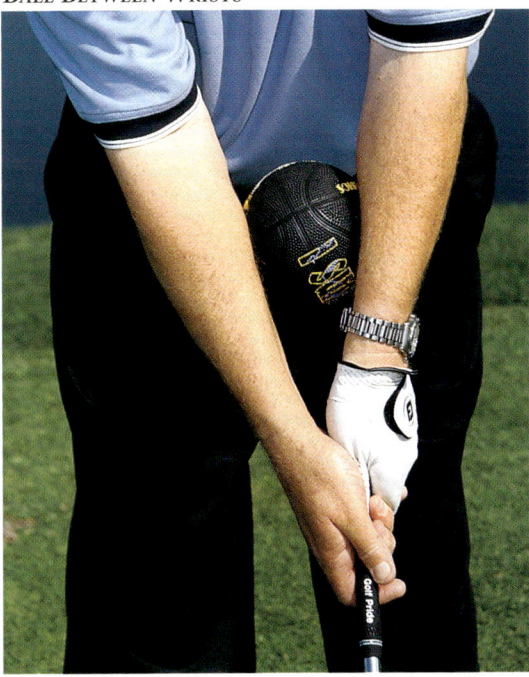

If the ball falls out at any part of the swing, you know immediately that you need some additional work to keep the ball in place. Improvement comes by not fortifying old swing flaws, but by practicing the correct techniques.

BALL STAYS BETWEEN WRISTS

As you swing, the ball remains in place all the way through the swing. For illustration purposes, I'm only demonstrating three positions that concern downswing through impact.

Downswing to Impact

125

IMPACT

IRON SHADOW DRILL

This drill helps you develop an angle of attack for iron play that allows you to hit the ball before taking a divot. The key is having a target line to aim for. It's okay to hit the ball and the ground at the same time, or to hit the ground slightly after the ball (your shots will be lower), but you should never hit the ground before hitting the ball.

Martin demonstrates that when hitting irons the vast majority of your divot must be on the target side of the ball.

IRON PRACTICE LINE DIVOTS

Another way to maximize the shadow drill experience is to just use the line without a ball. Try to see how many times you can create a divot that starts on the line. Adjusting your stance in response to the divot's club entry point also helps develop an understanding for correct ball position.

- Divot too far forward = Adjust so the line is marginally back in your stance. Make small changes, not large ones.

- Divot too far back = Adjust so the line is marginally forward in your stance. Again, make only small adjustments to fine-tune.

1-SETUP

Once again I'm using the sun to my advantage. I connected two shafts together and placed them on the sunny side of the ball so as to cast a straight-line shadow. Spray paint or a string will also work. Notice the shadow line is up against the back of the ball.

2-SHADOW GUIDES YOU

This action photo shows the correct angle of attack to bring the clubface into contact with the inside back quadrant of the ball at impact. The shadow line is my guide.

DRIVER SHADOW PRACTICE LINE DRILL

Use the shadow line to practice the correct angle for your driver shaft at impact. While you can't hit balls for this drill, the key is that the shaft and shadow line should be overlapping at impact. Irons should have an 8- to 10-degree target-forward angle, but good players have their driver shafts vertical at impact, which would be parallel to the shadow.

IMPACT

SPLIT GRIP ENERGY DRILL

Transfer all the energy down the shaft and out to the head of the club at impact. Make sure the clubface is closing as you go through the hit. The amount you pull with your left hand and the amount you push with your right hand should be equal.

- If you pull too much with the left hand but not enough with the right hand, you will leak balls to the right.

- If you push too much with the right hand but do not pull enough with the left hand, you will hit balls to the left.

Placing your index finger down the back of the shaft will let you feel that it's pointing directly at the ball when you hit it. It should also point at the target when the shaft reaches a hip-high, parallel-to-the-ground position after impact.

Martin splits his grip to demonstrate this drill.

1-Backswing Split Grip

A good view of the split grip. The index finger points toward the sky.

2-Split the Grip/Point the Finger

At setup, do not overlap or interlock the grip. Instead, split the grip so the hands do not touch. Point the right index finger down the back of the shaft. Back of the shaft means the side away from the ball.

3-Impact

At impact the index finger should point at the ball (arrow).

4-Point Finger at Target

As the shaft reaches the important hip-high checkpoint, when it's parallel to the ground, your index finger should point directly at the target.

DRAG THE BAG DRILL

Develop the feeling of dragging the shaft through the hitting zone, and your hands will automatically be slightly ahead at impact.

The best way to develop the dragging-the-shaft feeling is to actually drag a weighted object through the hitting area. In this case, a bag of range balls is put to good use. Notice how my hands are slightly ahead at what would be the impact point (2).

Downswing to Impact

127

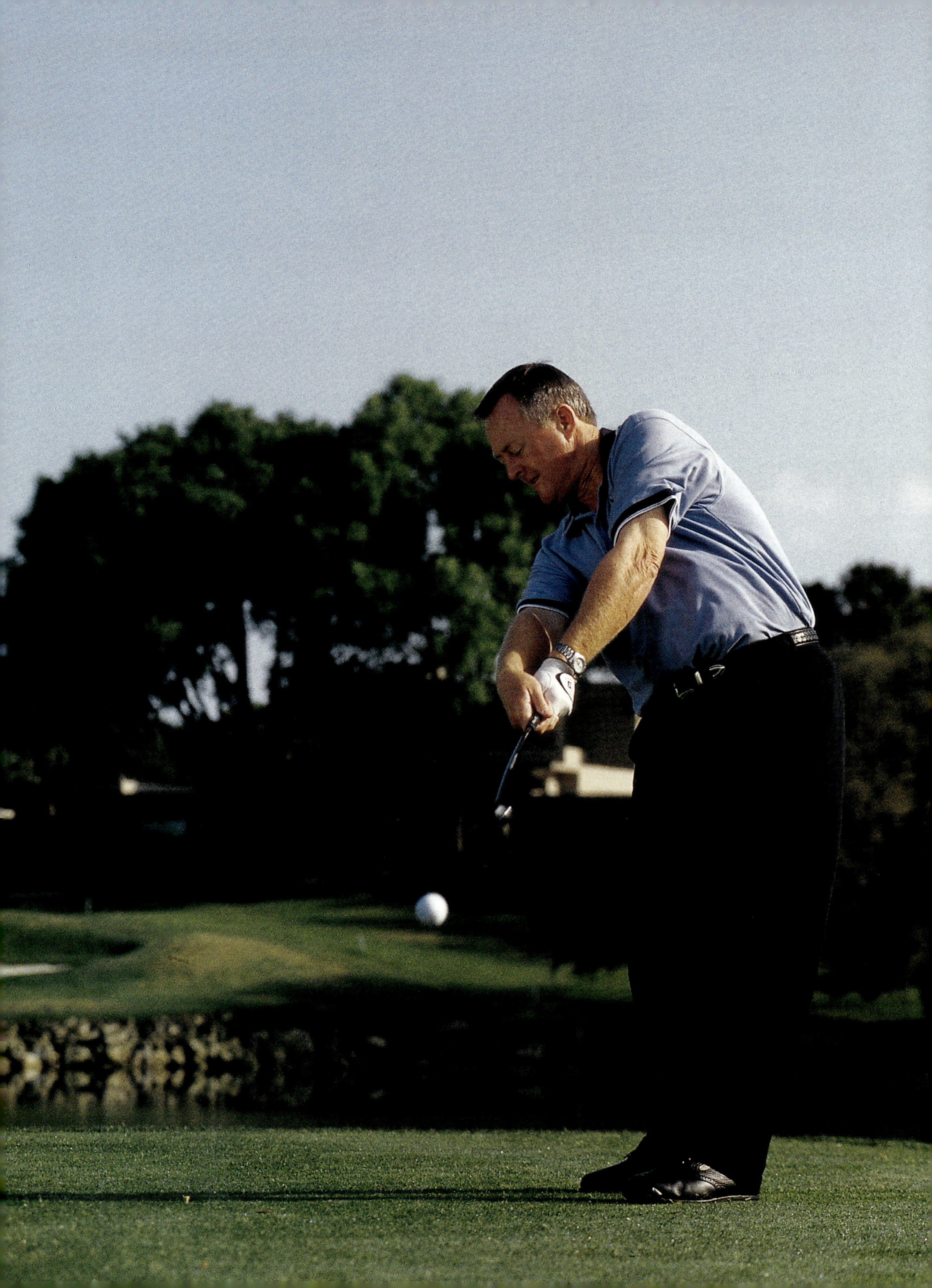

8 PAST IMPACT TO FINISH

Follow-through should be the result of what has gone on before!—Martin Hall

What difference does follow-through make since the ball has already left the clubface? Think of it in terms of bookends or like joining two points together.

A swing that is correct at the hip-height position on the downswing and as equally correct at hip height on the follow-through will likely be correct at impact. But it's a lot easier to feel certain things at follow-through than at impact.

After impact, a clubhead slows down, and as it goes up the swing plane it slows down even more. As a result, feeling where the hands and club are at hip height on the follow-through is much easier than trying to get the same feeling on the downswing or at impact.

With the focus still on the all-important impact position, this chapter provides the insight and drills you'll need to continue on the correct swing plane after hitting the ball.

THREE KEYS FOR SUCCESS

Programming your mind for changes in the follow-through will often change ball flight for the better. I suppose the reason has more to do with starting the swing with that intent, rather than hitting the ball and trying to actually do something specific on the follow-through. In reality, you have to do something different before you even swing the clubhead to the ball to ensure a good follow-through. There are three questions you always need to keep in mind:

1. What direction are you swinging the club? To the left, right or toward the target?

2. Where is the clubface at impact? Is it pointing to the left, right or toward the target? Hip-height positions on the downswing and follow-through provide the answer.

3. Are you compressing the ball at impact? Swinging in the correct direction, having your clubface pointing down the target line at impact, and compressing the ball with a solid hit, turns you into a very good player.

STRAIGHT ARMS AFTER IMPACT

CHICKEN WING

The arms are not ramrod straight in this weak chicken-wing follow-through.

If impact occurs at a 6 o'clock position, then just after impact both arms should be ramrod straight as they point with the club to 5 o'clock. What keeps the arms straight past impact? The slight pushing together of the elbows practiced earlier, with a ball placed between the wrists.

One of the keys to compressing the ball is to have both arms as straight as they can possibly be just after impact. It's the only place during the golf swing where they are both straight.

PRACTICE THE FOLLOW-THROUGH

Are you one of those golfers whose practice swing concerns itself mainly with the backswing and downswing? When it comes to following through, do you give it a halfhearted attempt?

I would rather see golfers concentrate more on their forward swing from the top, all the way down and through, than be so overly concerned about the backswing. Programming your brain and body for the correct balance and acceleration of your forward swing provides the positive information you need for success.

Clubhead Rotation

FULL ROLL

While some people prefer to talk in terms of wrist release, I think your understanding is ratcheted up if you think about what the face of the club is doing as a result of certain actions like wrist roll. Here are three different possibilities, and each has a specific purpose.

At this position past impact, the arms are straight and the thumbs are over the top of the shaft. The face is likewise affected and closes after impact. While this is not a suggested post-impact position for golfers who presently hook their shots, the advantages of this position are:

- Maximum power for hitting the ball as far as you can.

- Works to eliminate slicing for anybody with that flight pattern tendency.

- Ideal for golfers who are not strong.

HALF ROLL

REVERSE ROLL

This is a good position for accuracy. Holding on by not allowing the wrists to develop a full rotation is the way to achieve this half-roll position. The thumbs are more on the side of the shaft. Comparing this clubface with the full roll position reveals it has not closed as much. The advantages are:

- Accuracy.

- Creating a slight fade trajectory to shape a specific shot.

Slicers should avoid this position because it enhances slicing the ball. For some golfers, however, this can be advantageous for hitting specific shots. The thumbs are underneath the shaft, preventing both the wrist from rolling over and the clubface from closing. The advantages for preventing clubface rotation past impact are:

- Playing a slice to fly the ball around trouble or to get it to a specific target.

- Playing a very high lob shot.

Past Impact to Finish

Drill

Clubhead Rotation

Rotation Drill

This drill, using a full bucket of water, helps develop the full roll for a powerful swing.

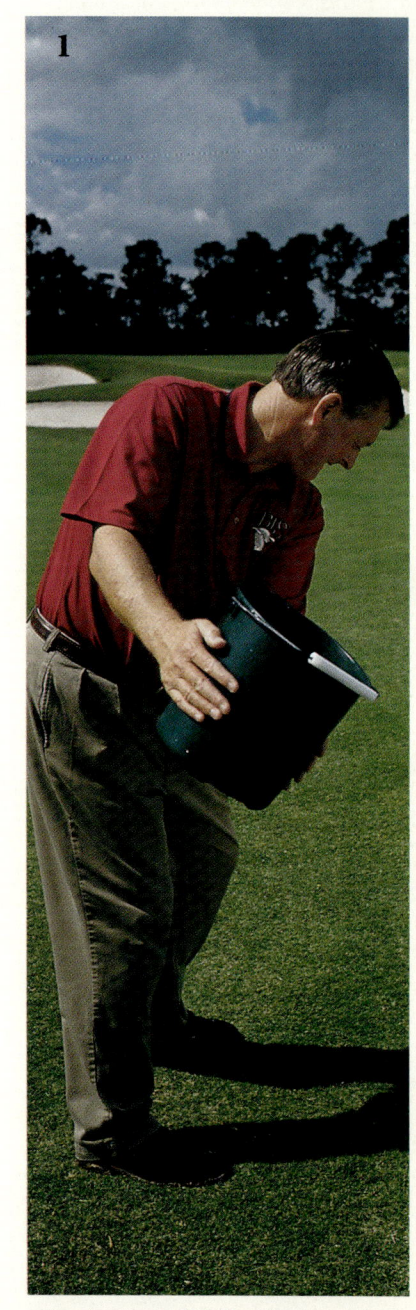

1

Fill a bucket half full with water. As you maintain your balance position, slowly swing back to the position seen here.

2

To develop the full roll, swing forward through the impact area with the image of tossing the water behind your left shoulder.

3

Rotate your right arm over your left to follow through, tossing the water behind your left shoulder. Concentrate on feeling this same rotation during your golf swing to maximize your distance or avoid slicing.

Drills

Johnny Miller Recoil Drills

Let's give some credit to Johnny Miller, who has one of the sharpest minds I've ever listened to. His insights into the game are outstanding, as demonstrated in the next three drills that will train your ball flight using *follow-through recoil*. Recoil means bringing the shaft back in front after the follow-through. The angle of the shaft, as you recoil, definitely helps shape the shot.

Straight Shot Follow-Through

Shot Flight

Follow-Through and Recoil

With the straight shot (left), you swing through to the finish position (1) and then bring the shaft down.

- Notice how the shaft is almost vertical (2).

- The elbows feel level and the shoulders have only a slight tilt, so the right shoulder is just slightly lower than the left.

JOHNNY MILLER RECOIL DRILLS

Draw Follow-Through

SHOT FLIGHT

FOLLOW-THROUGH AND RECOIL

With the draw (left), the right arm rolling over the left creates a closing clubface rotation, so that at the finish, the right arm is over the left (1). Then bring the shaft down in front.

- The shaft is at an oblique angle with the right arm over the left (2).

- The right shoulder is higher than it would be for the straight shot.

Golf Myths Exposed

JOHNNY MILLER RECOIL DRILLS

FADE FOLLOW-THROUGH

SHOT FLIGHT

FOLLOW-THROUGH AND RECOIL

1

2

With the fade (left), the clubface rotation was held back. This follow-through position mimics how the great Ben Hogan looked at this position. The shaft wraps somewhat around the back of the head (1). Then bring the shaft down in front.

- The shaft is at an opposite angle than of a draw (2).

- The right shoulder will be lower than it was for the straight shot.

Past Impact to Finish

Drills

Past Impact to Finish

Hide the Left Leg Drill

Good

A good mental image is to try hiding your left leg at the finish from someone who is watching you from across your ball, as seen from this view.

Bad

This is the incorrect finish position, showing a golfer who pushes the ball to the right. Notice the left leg is certainly not hidden.

Elbows Point Down

A Good Finish Thought

While not a swing fixer, completing your swing with your elbows pointing down is a good image to have.

PAST IMPACT TO FINISH

TEE ON LEFT SHOE DRILL

This demanding drill verifies whether you stay balanced all the way through the swing to follow-through. Place a tee on the top of your left foot and keep the tee pointing upward from start to finish, all the way through your swing.

If you try to overpower the shot, you'll lose balance, causing the tee to fall as your foot moves in a survival attempt to keep you upright.

TEE UP

Place a tee pointing to the sky on top of your left foot (inset). Start your golf swing from a balanced position that is maintained all the way to follow-through. The tee should stay on.

SWING THROUGH

The tee continues to point to the sky as a result of a balanced swing (inset). Lunging at the ball or losing your balance at any time will cause the tee to fall.

ANTI-ROLL DRILL

This is a more extreme version of the tee drill, to help cure a problem some golfers have: wanting to roll onto the outside of the left foot at the swing's finish. This problem makes you get way in front of the ball at impact, causing pushed shots. Placing a shaft under the outside of the left foot is a very good way to practice finishing with your weight on the inside of the foot.

PLACE THE SHAFT

Place the shaft of a club under the left side of your left foot. This makes it difficult to roll over to the outside of the foot during the swing.

CORRECT FINISH

The shaft under the edge develops the feeling of finishing the swing correctly on the inside of the left foot.

Past Impact to Finish

SECTION III
TIME FOR DESSERT

With all its difficulty, golf is still just a game. So remember to enjoy it. When you reach this section you've worked very hard, taken one bite of new knowledge at a time and digested it. The drills helped to fortify your understanding of what golf is really all about.

Chances are you've never thought about what the face of your club is doing as you swing, but you will from now on because that's the only real way to correct any new flaws that might creep in. You've had the vegetables, so now it's time to savor the dessert that knowledge can bring you.

You're prepared for Chapter 9, "Golf's Only Secret," and then for a final look on turning fiction into fact in Chapter 10.

IN THIS SECTION

GOLF'S ONLY SECRET

- Clubface Square at Impact
- Shaft is Five Times Parallel
- Clubface Rotates 270 Degrees
- The Power Punch

CHANGING FICTION TO FACTS

- Curing a Slice
- Maintaining a Steady Head
- Eliminating Fat Shots
- Correctly Finishing the Swing

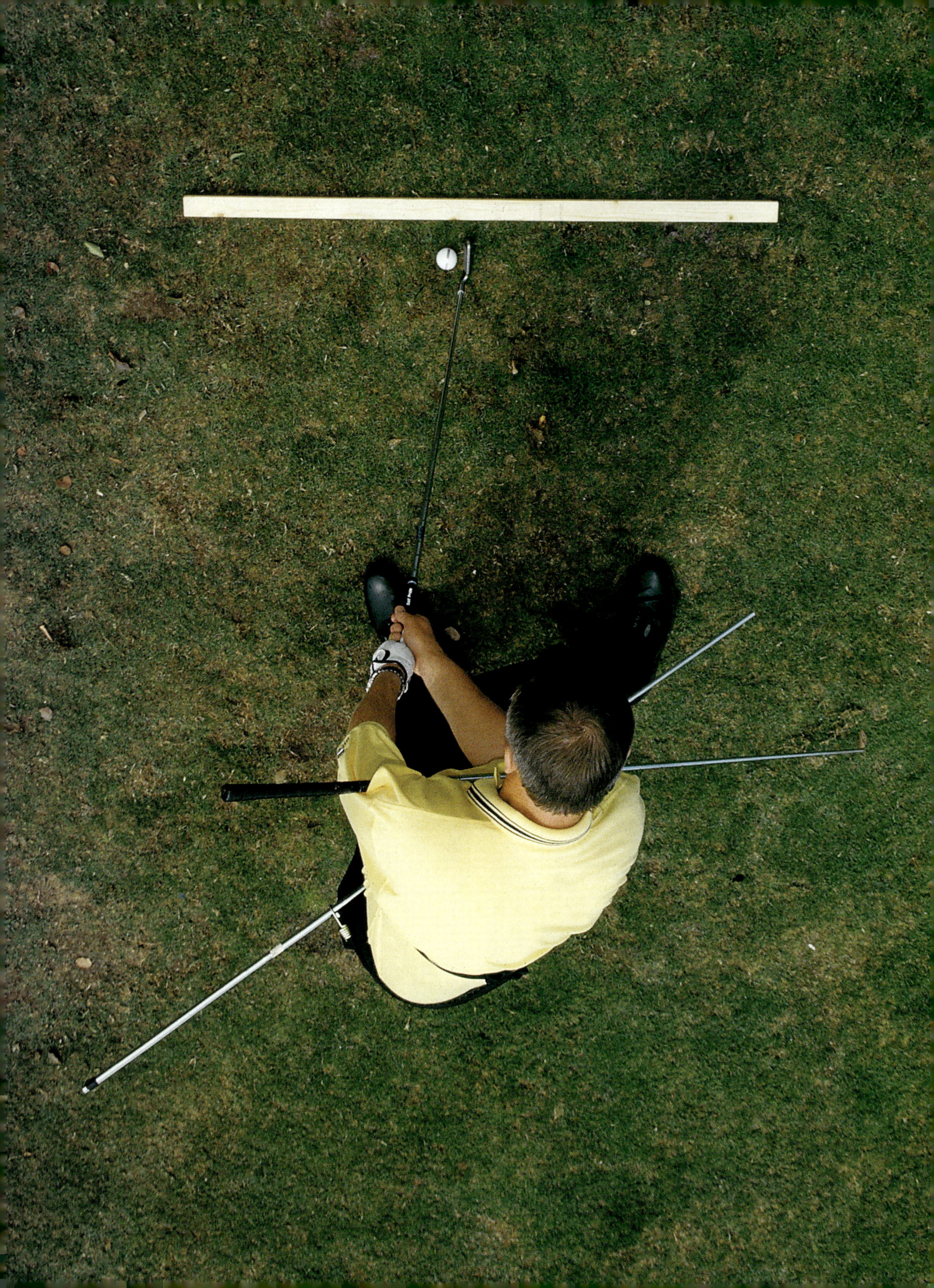

9 Golf's Only Secret:
Square at Impact

"When I swing straight, my ball will go crooked. When I swing crooked, my ball can go straight. Crooked means an arc."
—Martin Hall

Throughout this book I have tried to correct the myths and misconceptions that prevent you from making any real improvement in your game. Quite often these myths and misconceptions are implemented in your game because you received poor advice or direction. As golfers, we can all be very gullible at vulnerable times, and willing to grab at any seemingly reasonable *rescue line*.

As a teacher, I understand that. But the bottom line is that in golf the only thing that really matters at all is that *your ball goes straight!* The only purpose of the golf swing is to deliver your clubface squarely and truly to the golf ball. The face must be square at impact to hit the ball along the target line.

This chapter provides a summary for all you've learned so far, and includes a few drills to help you put it all together. The main thrust is perfecting the *move within the move:* correct clubface rotation during the swing. *That* is golf's only real secret!

Important Swing Check Positions

When I ask students what it is they would like to get out of a lesson, they usually respond, "I want to be more consistent." The problem is they may already be consistent, but it's consistently bad. What they really mean is they want to get better.

The only way to become consistently good is to change your swing so that a square-to-the-line clubface sweet spot smashes into the ball at impact. Chapter 3 presented the sweet spot test that you should use to occasionally monitor your progress.

As you work on your swing there are some important check positions that ensure your clubface is rotating properly on the swing plane. The drills throughout the book are designed to help you learn to swing the club correctly.

Hitting the center of the ball at the sweet spot of a square-to-the-line clubface is the only way to consistently play better golf. Martin's drive will head straight down his target line.

Parallel and Square

Anytime your shaft becomes parallel to the ground it must also be parallel to the target line. This happens five times during your full swing (see page 143). A lot of players don't take a full swing and consequently cannot get the club to parallel at the top of the backswing. For them, the shaft might only be parallel four times. Three of those times the club shaft is also hip high.

BACKSWING

FORWARD SWING

As I swing back and the shaft becomes parallel to the ground at hip high, it is also parallel to my target line. When I swing down toward the ball the club must also be in this same plane. Notice how the shaft of the club is parallel to the target line.

In chapter 8, I offered an observation that a follow-through was like bookends. Here, as the club reaches the hip-high position past impact, it is once again parallel to the ground and parallel to the target. Notice how the shaft of the driver is parallel to the ball's flight.

SQUARE AT IMPACT

At the exact moment of impact the club arrives at the ball with the face pointing directly down the target line. Because we swing along a tilted oval with no straight lines, this is the only moment when the clubface is pointing directly at the target. Notice how the ball is right in the center of the club.

The large photo that started this chapter shows the impact positions of my shoulders and hips as seen from above. Here is what you want to see and feel:

- The shoulders are parallel to the target line.

- The hips have already turned past parallel, clearing out of the way.

- The arms and hands have plenty of room to powerfully swing the on-plane clubhead through the impact zone.

- My engine has stayed ahead of the caboose.

Shaft Five Times Parallel, Clubface Rotates 270 Degrees

During a golf swing that correctly positions the shaft parallel to the target line five times (whenever the club is parallel to the ground), the clubface will rotate a total of 270 degrees.

Ninety degrees of rotation comes on the backswing, and 180 degrees of rotation on the downswing-through-impact to follow-through, for a combined total of 270 degrees. With all of this rotation that must occur, your face is only square to the target line for a fraction of a second at impact.

1-Backswing

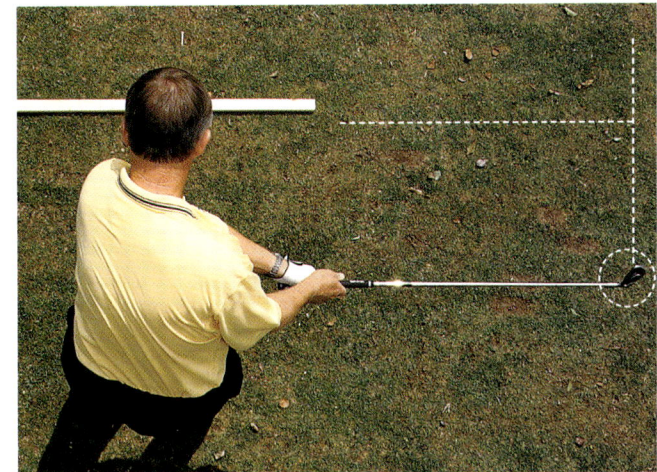

- Shaft parallel to ground and target line.
- 90-degree leading edge of clubface rotation from the target line.

2-Top of Backswing

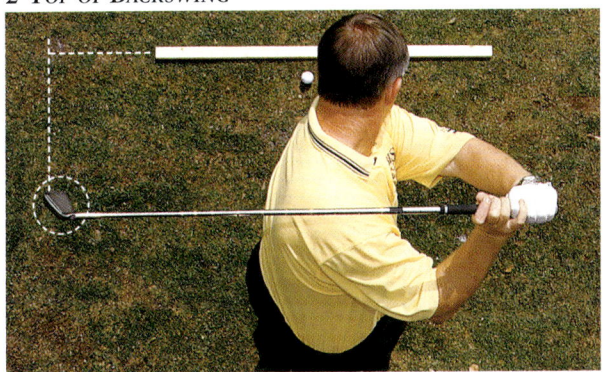

- Shaft parallel to ground and target line.
- 90-degree angle of the leading edge of clubface to the target line.

3-Downswing

The clubface rotates 90 degrees back to impact and another 90 degrees to follow-through for a downswing total of 180 degrees.

- Shaft parallel to ground and target line.
- 90-degree leading edge of clubface angle to the target line.

4-Past Impact

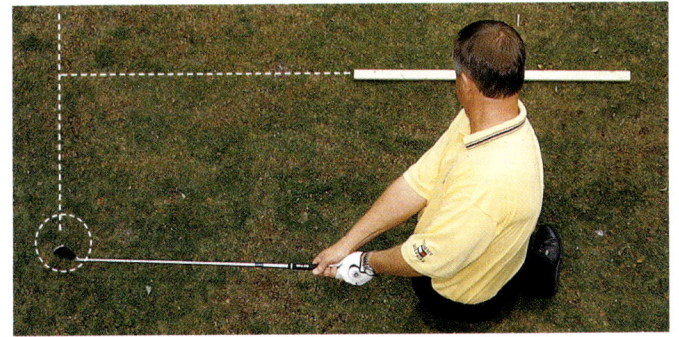

From the downswing hip-high position to this hip-high position, the clubface rotates 180 degrees. Impact is when the clubface is square to the target line.

- Shaft parallel to ground and target line.
- 90-degree leading edge of clubface rotation from the target line.

5-Follow-Through

- Shaft almost parallel to the target line. The optimum position should be parallel, but that's why I teach for a living!
- 90-degree leading edge of clubface angle from the target line.

Golf's Only Secret

143

DRILLS

SQUARE AT IMPACT

THUMBS UP DRILL

Sometimes it's good to have big picture images of what makes the golf swing work. In such a complex sport, having a simple image or thought can do a lot for your game. Thumb up to thumb up is a perfect example of a simple thought and image that keeps the clubhead on plane.

Backswing

Follow-Through

Take a few practice swings visualizing your left thumb pointing to the sky during your backswing (left), and your right thumb pointing to the sky as you follow through (right). Next, hit some practice balls with the same preprogrammed feeling. This is also an excellent drill to incorporate into your practice swings during an actual round on the course.

THE DRILLS AND YOUR PRACTICE SWINGS

Try incorporating one or more of these drills into your practice swing. The hope is that preprogramming your brain and muscle memory will facilitate some transfer of the drill when you are actually swinging at the ball. If your game goes off during the round, as it does to even the best players in the world, your newly developed understanding of the golf swing should help you select a drill to correct a fault that may have infiltrated your swing.

RIGHT AND LEFT ARM FOLD DRILL

This drill relaxes some of the tension out of your joints, adding freedom into your swing motion. Although your elbows are gently pushed together so they can't be pulled apart, they shouldn't be rigid.

You need a fine blend of enough strength to keep the elbows together, and enough relaxation to ensure your arms aren't so tight that the right elbow can't fold on the backswing and the left elbow can't fold on the forward swing.

This drill also improves your hand-eye coordination and your tempo.

1-RIGHT ARM FOLD SETUP

Begin by holding the club in the right hand and placing your left hand under the right forearm.

IS THERE A DOMINANT ARM?

Another misconception is that the left arm should be the dominant arm in the swing. I don't believe there is a dominant arm in the golf swing. The biggest difference between poor players and good players is not what they do with the left arm, *but what they do with the right arm.* The right arm is not dominant, but good players don't let the right arm bend all that much going back. Don't make the mistake of over-thinking what the left arm should do and under-thinking what the right arm should do.

2-RIGHT ARM FOLD

Use this drill only in practice. Swing back and through, continuing to hold the left hand on the right arm. The drill helps fold the right arm on the backswing, setting the club correctly at the top of the swing plane. When hitting balls with the drill, always use a tee.

3-LEFT ARM FOLD

Reverse the drill by holding the left arm with the right hand as you swing. The key to this drill is to help get the left arm to fold on the follow-through. Intending to fold the arm over actually helps it to turn over and square the club at impact.

Power Punch

This is golf's knockout punch. You can watch a great boxer's knockout punch and think it just came from his right arm. But it didn't. It came from his hips, legs and the right arm, just like a piston. Boom!

Tiger Woods epitomizes this whenever he bashes one with his driver. Just like Ben Hogan, his left leg snaps straight just as his right arm snaps straight. Coordinating these two movements is the power punch, which occurs through and just after impact.

Power Punch in Action

Martin demonstrates the power punch, which occurs through and just after impact. The left leg and right arm snap straight like a piston. Boom!

Practicing the Power Punch

You can train yourself to feel the power punch. Start by hitting half shots with a 7-iron and the ball on the ground so as to take a nice chunky divot. The key is to try stopping the club when the right arm is straight as you see in the photo.

1 - Take the club back halfway.

2 - Transition to your downswing.

3 - Swing slow enough so that you can feel both your left leg straighten at the knee and your right arm straighten at the elbow.

4 - Try to freeze this power punch position to get that feeling.

5 - If you have a runaway caboose, you won't be able to stop because you're slapping your wrists at the ball. Always have the engine (your body) going as fast as the caboose (your hands).

Head on Pillow

To keep the correct shoulder tilt throughout the shot, visualize your head resting on a pillow at the finish of the swing. If your head wobbles, your balance will be upset as your eyes and fluid in the ears send out conflicting signals to your brain.

Ken Venturi always points out that the great players finish their swings with the right ear closer to the ground than their left. The "head on the pillow" finish is an excellent image, especially when hitting irons. You should be able to look at the flight of the ball from underneath.

Think about this image: After the swing, your right ear should be closer to the ground than your left.

Golf's Only Secret

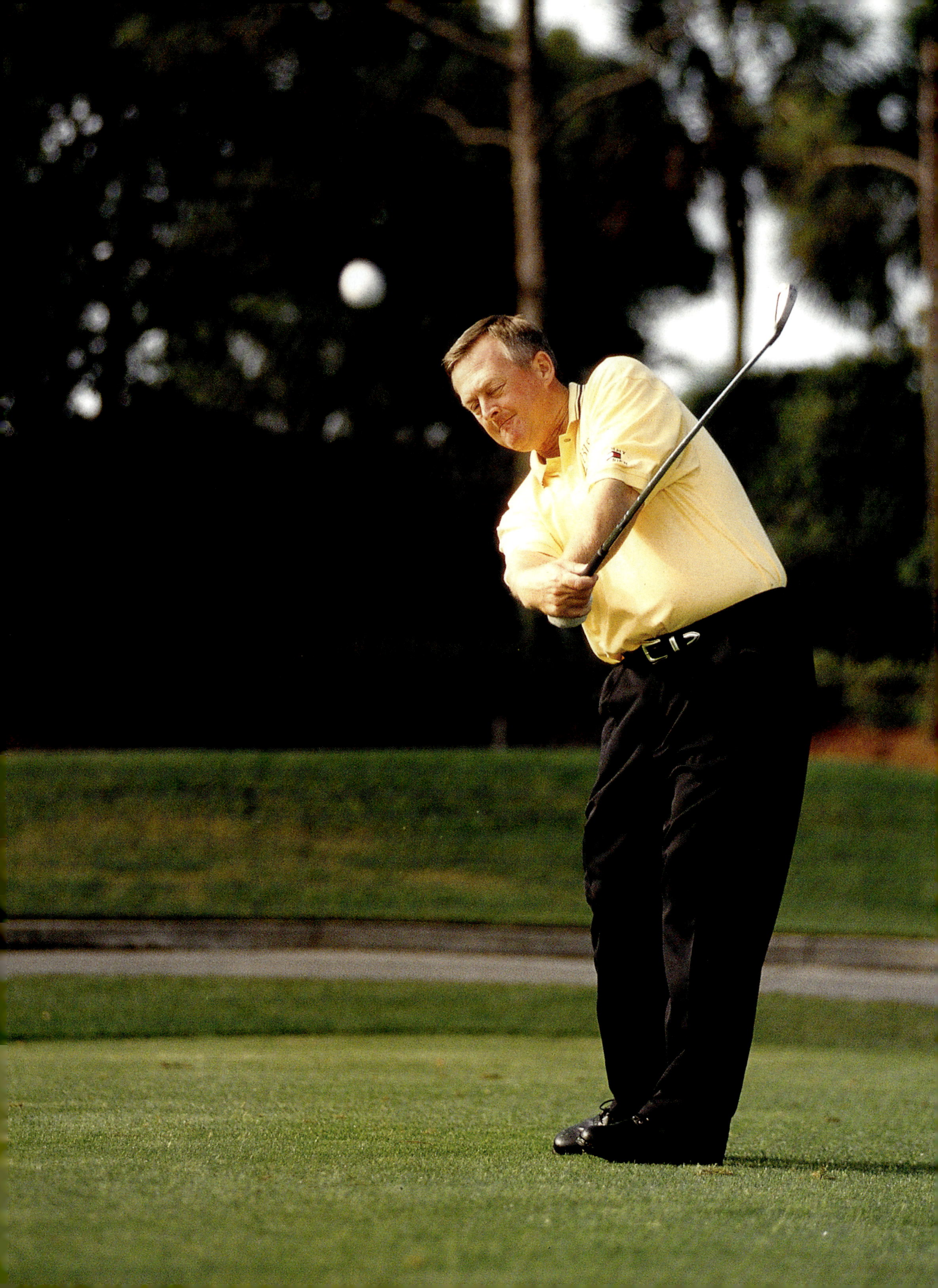

10 CHANGING FICTION TO FACTS

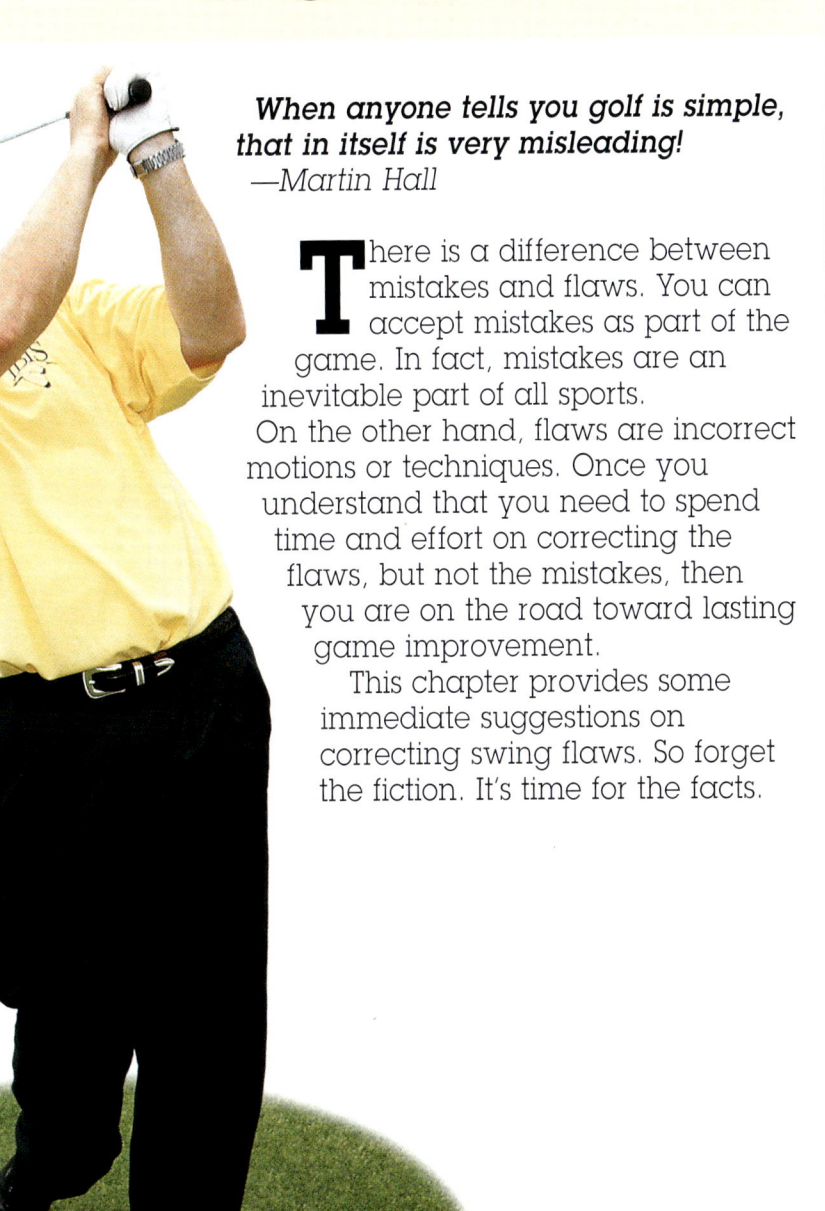

When anyone tells you golf is simple, that in itself is very misleading!
—Martin Hall

There is a difference between mistakes and flaws. You can accept mistakes as part of the game. In fact, mistakes are an inevitable part of all sports.

On the other hand, flaws are incorrect motions or techniques. Once you understand that you need to spend time and effort on correcting the flaws, but not the mistakes, then you are on the road toward lasting game improvement.

This chapter provides some immediate suggestions on correcting swing flaws. So forget the fiction. It's time for the facts.

Curing a Slice

Slices come from clubfaces that are open at impact. So somewhere during your swing you have to do something to close the clubface. The next two tips work on changing the clubface, and the third tip adjusts the swing for a new clubface position.

Strengthen Your Grip

Your grip directly affects clubface positions during the swing. Slicers tend to have weak grips, where the V's of both hands, formed by the thumb and index finger, point to the left side of the torso. To strengthen your grip, point the V's to the inside of the right shoulder.

Left Hand

Right Hand

Holding the club out in front, notice how the left-hand V (arrow) points to the inside of my right shoulder.

Place the right hand on the club so that the V points to the inside of the right shoulder. This strengthens your grip and changes the position of your clubface during the swing (arrows), giving it a better chance of arriving square to the target line at impact.

Clubface Looks at the Ball

The early phase of your swing is important for starting the club away from the ball along the correct path. Make it simple, and work on keeping the clubface looking at the ball as it swings away. The clubface should *never* be looking at the sky at any time during the takeaway.

Takeaway

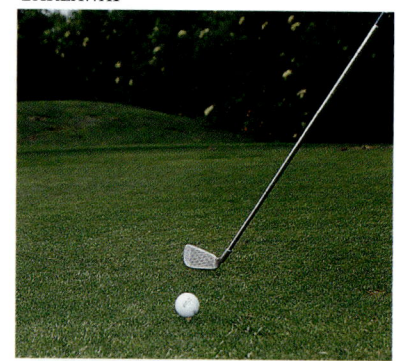

As the face of the club swings away from the ball it should continue looking at it for as long as possible. *The face never looks at the sky.*

SWING FEELS LOW TO HIGH

Grip and takeaway adjustments have changed what the face of the club does in the swing. So you probably need to make a little change in the path of the swing to allow for the new clubface position. Slicers tend to swing to the left of their target, also referred to as *out to in:* That's also a swing that goes from high to low. You need to create the feeling that the swing is now going from low to high.

FEEL THIS SWING

TOM FINISHES HIGH

Although it's just a feeling to correct a previous high-to-low slicing swing, try to feel the swing's new angle of attack and follow-through: it goes from low to high. Strive to feel that your clubhead is lower to the ground prior to impact, and that you finish with your hands high. I call it the Tom Lehman look (right).

Partners Club President Tom Lehman finishes his swing with his hands high, as Martin suggests for changing your high-to-low swing to the feeling of swinging low to high.

WHEN YOU'VE GONE FAR ENOUGH

One of the tricks about making corrections is knowing when you have gone far enough. As an example, Ibis, the club I teach at in Florida, is six miles west of Interstate 95.

If you asked me how to get to Interstate 95 from Ibis I would say, "You go out of Ibis and turn right." Common sense should tell you that if you just keep going you're going to end up in the ocean off Palm Beach. You have to know when you have gone far enough.

Just like you have to know when you've gone past the I-95 entrance, the same thing is true when making corrections. So if you were slicing the ball, made some corrections and are now hooking it, you have to understand that you must back off some of the changes until you have the ball flight just the way you want it.

That's why you must be attentive to what the ball is doing. Harvey Penick would tell his students, "Take just one aspirin but not the whole bottle." You always work off of your ball flight. I don't buy this stuff that golfers can make a perfect swing and not take any notice of where the ball is going.

Changing Fiction to Facts

Drills

Changing Fiction to Facts

Head Movement Drill

The only head that really comes up, causing a thin shot, is the clubhead. Golfers don't really look up too early. It's a case of the caboose getting ahead of the engine again. The real problem is that either the left wrist has broken down prior to impact, or the elbows have come apart. This drill helps correct that flaw.

1-Bungie Around Neck

Place a loop of bungie cord around your neck and a loop of plastic tape around your left thumb so that the cord is slack with your hand in front of your chest.

2-Push Your Hands Out

You want to feel your hands pushing out during the swing, which is what you must do in this drill to tighten the bungie cord.

3-Good Impact

The cord remains tight at impact as the hand leads. Notice the left wrist has not broken and the arms are straight.

4-Bad Impact

The slack cord proves immediately that my arms collapsed. Notice the left wrist angle. Remember golf's power punch? Through impact and early follow-through, the right arm snaps straight at the same time the left leg snaps straight, delivering a powerful wallop to the golf ball. After that, the left elbow can bend, allowing the swing to come up and around.

CHANGING FICTION TO FACTS

FAT SHOTS DRILL

1- TEE A BALL

Tee a ball just on the instep of your right foot, near the ankle.

Fat shots are not caused by taking your eyes off the ball, as the Helpful Henrys of the world would have you believe. David Duval and Annika Sorenstam, two of the best hitters golf has ever had, never even look at the ball at impact. Their eyes are down the fairway.

If you hit fat shots you most likely have your measurements wrong at impact. Why? Because you probably do not have proper leg and foot movement. I'll wager your legs tend to be as rock-solid as concrete.

The only time your legs should be rock-solid is for putting. Even as you chip, you want to roll onto the right instep at least a little bit.

For your long game, you need to train for some foot and knee movement to allow the club to lag behind and hit down on the ball. This drill does just that.

2- ANKLE KNOCKS BALL OFF TEE

Roll onto the right instep during your forward swing, knocking the ball off the tee with your ankle (inset).

Changing Fiction to Facts

153

CHANGING FICTION TO FACTS

CORRECTLY FINISHING THE SWING DRILL

AWFUL FINISH!

If the photo at right is how your finish looks, and friends tell you your shot was terrible because you didn't finish your swing, the reason is the right wrist. Your body didn't move very much through the shot because the right wrist flapped through the hit.

By keeping your right wrist bent, you keep your body engaged in the shot. Anytime the right wrist stays bent the body will keep moving, and anytime the right wrist becomes straight the body will stop moving immediately. This drill helps correct that flaw.

The Helpful Henrys of the world will tell you, "You didn't finish your swing!".

BOTTLE DRILL

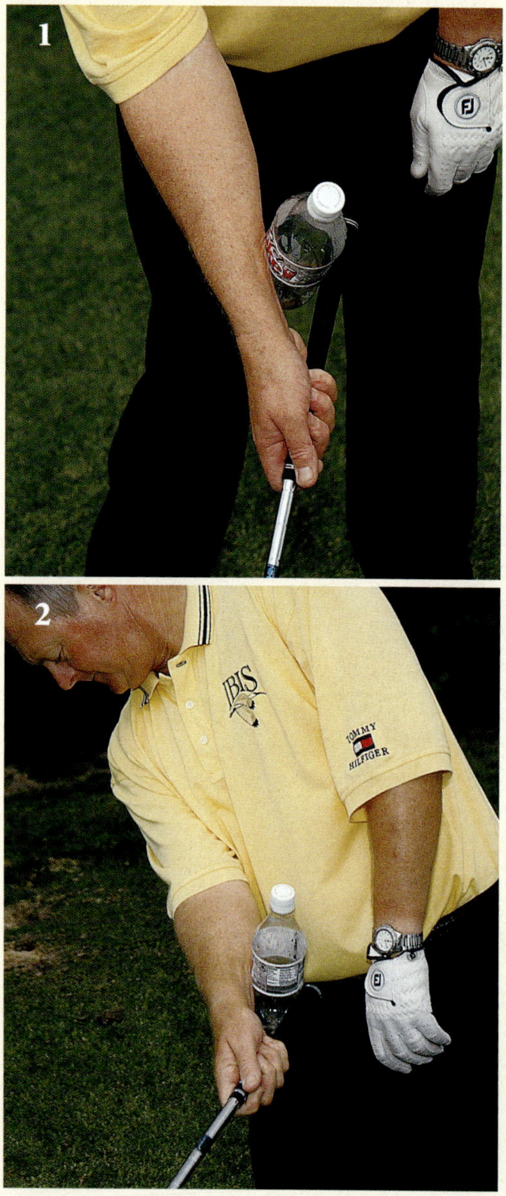

WRIST BRIDGE

Place a small empty plastic bottle between the grip and right wrist (1) to set the correct wrist bend you need during the swing (2) to keep the body engaged. Swing without crushing the bottle.

If the flaw develops or revisits during a round, make a few practice swings while keeping four fingers of your left hand between the right wrist and the grip to create the correct wrist bend. Do not crush your fingers while doing this! This re-programs your brain to get the body engaged and moving through the shot again.

CHANGING FICTION TO FACTS

FINISH FLAW DRILLS

Earlier in the book we dealt with how important it is to have a sense of symmetry in your golf swing. If your hands are over your right shoulder going back, then they should be over your left shoulder going through. It has to match to hit the ball straight. Here are some drills to develop golf swing symmetry.

HITCHHIKER DRILL

Make a few practice swings without a club and stick your thumb out like a hitchhiker. The finish position with the right thumb over the left shoulder is shown here, but to practice and develop a symmetrical swing the left thumb should also have gone over the right shoulder on the backswing.

TOO HIGH

I've seen many students in this too-high finish position. This drill helps correct the flaw.

SYMMETRY DRILL

After doing the hitchhiker drill a few times, hit some balls while you concentrate on having your hands go over your right shoulder on the backswing (1) and over the left shoulder (2) on the follow-through.

Epilogue

Having read this book from cover to cover, I hope that you've picked up some nuggets of information. These are things I've learned over 25 years of teaching.

Obviously, don't take every piece of information and try to incorporate it into next Saturday morning's game or they will have to haul you off to a mental institution very quickly! And, by all means, never listen to the *Helpful Henrys* and their portfolio of bad advice and misconceptions.

Here are some things to remember. If you are not improving, something has to change. To paraphrase Einstein, as we did earlier in the book: If you keep doing what you've been doing and expect a different result, you're going to be disappointed. One of my favorite quotes comes from Jim Rohn, a great business motivational speaker. He says, "It's not how fast you're moving, it's in what direction you are headed that counts."

The changes in your swing that I hope you will make as a result of what Steve and I have presented in this book may not be quick cures. But they will result in steady improvement. If you're not playing well, you'll find enough information and drills in this book to get you back on the correct road.

Here are some other thoughts to help:

- Cause and consequence are inseparable. Every action has a consequence.

- Practice does not make perfect. Practice makes permanent.

- What you practice becomes a part of you, and if you're not practicing the right stuff, then you won't get better, which is why I'm such a believer in drills.

I would like to thank the people who have helped me over the years to understand the golf swing to this point. I hope that you will learn something from this book as I have learned from the following great people. I'd like to thank John Jacobs from England, Bob Toski, Jim Flick, Peter Kostis, Chuck Cook, Chuck Evans, Ben Doyle and Homer Kelly for all of their efforts over the years with me.

Have fun while you improve. Golf is just a game, so enjoy it!

GLOSSARY

Address Your body position (posture, alignment, ball position) as you set up to the ball.

Addressing the Ball Taking a stance and grounding the club (except in a hazard) before taking a swing.

Approach A shot hit to the green.

Apron Slightly higher grassy area surrounding the putting surface. Also referred to as fringe.

Away A player who is farthest from the hole. This player plays his or her ball first.

Backspin The spin of a golf ball that is the opposite direction of the ball's flight.

Ball Mark The damaged, indented area in the ground caused by the ball when it lands on the green.

Ball Marker Something small to mark the position of your ball on the putting green. You should leave a marker when you remove your ball both to clean it and also to allow your playing partners to have an unobstructed line to the hole. Markers can be purchased and can be attached to your glove. You may also use a coin or similar object.

Birdie One stroke under the designated par of the hole.

Blade To hit the ball at its center with the bottom edge of your club.

Blocked Shot Hitting a ball on a straight line to the right.

Bogey One stroke over the designated par for a hole.

Bump and Run A type of approach shot that lands and then rolls onto the green and toward the hole.

Bunker Also referred to as a sand trap.

Carry How far a ball flies in the air. If a water hazard is in front of you, you have to figure the carry to be sure you've taken enough club.

Casual Water A temporary water accumulation not intended as a hazard. Consult the published *Rules of Golf* for information on the relief you are entitled to.

Chili-Dip Hitting the ground before contacting the ball. The result: weak, popped-up shots also called "fat."

Divot Turf displaced by a player's club when making a swing. Divots must be repaired.

Double Bogey Two strokes over the designated par for a hole.

Draw A shot that curves from right to left for right-handers and the opposite for left-handed golfers.

Drop The act of returning a ball back into play. Consult *The Rules of Golf* for correct information on circumstances where this occurs.

Eagle Two strokes under the designated par for a hole.

Fade A controlled, slight left-to-right ball flight pattern. Also can be called a cut.

Fairway Closely mowed route of play between tee and green.

Fore A warning cry to any person in the way of play or who may be within the flight of your ball.

Green The putting surface.

Gross Score Total number of strokes taken to complete a designated round.

Ground the Club Touching the surface of the ground with the sole of the club at address.

Halved the Hole The phrase used to describe a hole where identical scores were made.

Handicap A deduction from a player's gross score. Handicaps for players are determined by guidelines published by the USGA.

Honor The right to tee off first, earned by scoring the lowest on the previous hole.

Hook A stroke made by a right-handed player that curves the ball to the left of the target. It's just the opposite for left-handers.

Hosel The metal part of the clubhead where the shaft is connected.

Hot A ball that comes off the clubface without backspin and will go farther than normal as a result. If a lie puts grass between the clubface and ball, the grooves can't grip the ball to develop backspin. Understanding this, a golfer knows the ball will come out "hot" and plans for that.

Lateral Hazard A hazard (usually water) that is on the side of a fairway or green. Red stakes are used to mark lateral hazards.

Lie Stationary position of the ball. It is also described as the angle of the shaft in relation to the ground when the club sole rests naturally.

Local Rules Special rules for the course that you are playing.

Loft The amount of angle built into the clubface.

Match Play A format where each hole is a separate contest. The winner is the individual or team that wins more holes than are left to play.

Mulligan A second ball that's hit from the same location. The shot that's tried again. Limited to friendly, noncompetitive rounds.

Net Score Gross score less handicap.

Par The score a golfer should make on a given hole. Determined by factoring in 2 putts plus the number of strokes needed to cover the yardage between the tee and green.

Provisional Ball A second ball hit before a player looks for his or her first ball, which may be out of bounds or lost.

Pull Shot A straight shot in which the flight of the ball is left of the target for right-handers and right of the target for left-handers.

Push Shot A straight shot in which the flight of the ball is right of the target for a right-handed golfer and left of the target for a left-hander.

Rough Areas of longer grass adjacent to the tee, fairway green or hazards.

Shank To hit a shot off the club's hosel.

Slice A stroke made across the ball, creating spin that curves the ball to the right of the intended target for right-handed golfers and to the left of the target for left-handers.

Stance Position of the feet at address.

Stroke Any forward motion of the clubhead made with an intent to strike the ball. The number of strokes taken on each hole are entered for that hole's score.

Stroke Play Competition based on the total number of strokes taken.

Target The spot or area a golfer chooses for the ball to land or roll.

Top To hit the ball above its center.

Index

A
Anti-Roll drill, 137
Arc
  extension myth, 30–32
Arc drill, 21
Arm position
  dominant arm misconception, 145
  extension myth, 30–32
  Left Arm Check drill, 97
  left arm straight myth, 16–18
  Natural Swing Arc drill, 32
  past impact to finish, 130
  String drill, 18
  Takeaway Arm Extension drill, 93

B
Backswing, 87–105
  Clubface Looks at Ball drill, 96
  Crossed Shaft drill, 91
  Keep Hands Low drill, 94
  Left Arm Check drill, 97
  90-degree backswing rotation, 45
  Preset Wrist drill, 92
  swing inside to outside myth, 36
  swing straight back myth, 28–29
  symmetrical swing plane, 60
  Takeaway Arm Extension drill, 93
  Takeaway drill, 91
  Takeaway Slot drill, 95
  tempo, timing and rhythm, 89
  Tilted Circle drill, 29
  train/golf synergy, 88
  turn to keep club on plane, 23–25
  Windup Resistance drill, 90
Backswing coil
  Connection drill, 103
  Crossed Club Pivot drill, 100
  Nerf Ball drill, 101
  Pivot drill #1, 99
  Pivot drill #2, 99
  Regulate Hip Twist drill, 100
  Right Elbow in Front of the Body Drill, 105
  Right Wrist Bend drill, 104
  Shadow Coil drill, 102
  Turn in the Barrel drill, 98
Backyard Ball Position drill, 76
Balance, dynamic, 84–85
Balance Beam drill, 85
Balanced posture, 77–83
  balanced head, 82
  body tilt, 79
  check the hollow, 79
  Chin to Left Leg drill, 80
  chin up, 83
  Push the Right Hip drill, 81
  Right Shoulder Tilt drill, 81
  Scott McCarron's Balance Beam drill, 77–78
  set up in balance, 79
  weight check, 83
Ball position, 74–76
  Backyard Ball Position drill, 76
  draw, 75
  driving, 75
  fade, 75
  middle irons, 75
  short irons, 75
  swaying changes ball position, 74
Big Punch drill, 34

C
Chin to Left Leg drill, 80
Clubface
  Clubface Looks at Ball drill, 96
  square at impact, 6
  takeaway swing plane, 6
  top ten fundamentals for square, 68
  trapped behind myth, 40–41
Clubface Looks at Ball drill, 96
Clubhead
  Arc drill, 21
  heel hit, 62–63
  hooking position, 47
  hook-producing chain reaction, 50–51
  keep clubhead low to ground myth, 19–21
  maintain radius of swing, 20
  90-degree backswing rotation, 45
  180-degree downswing rotation, 46
  Rotation drill, 132
  rotation past impact to finish, 131
  slice-producing chain reaction, 48–49
  slicing position, 47
  square at impact, 44
  sweet spot, 62–63
  swing checkpoints for, 47
  Swing Plane Sweet Spot drill, 63
  toe hit, 62–63
  270 degrees of rotation, 44–51, 143
Compression drill, 122
Connection drill, 103
Correctly Finishing the Swing drill, 154
Crossed Club Pivot drill, 100
Crossed Shaft drill, 91

D
Downswing. See also Downswing to Impact
  180-degree downswing rotation, 46
  swing inside to outside myth, 36
  symmetrical swing plane, 61
Downswing to Impact, 117–127
  Compression drill, 122
  Drag the Bag drill, 127
  Driver Shadow Practice Line drill, 126
  Energy Transfer drill, 124
  Foot Police drill, 123
  Gardner Dickinson drill, 120–121
  Gentle Elbow Push drill, 125
  Iron Shadow drill, 126
  iron vs. driver shaft angles, 118
  Martin's key to power golf, 118
  "Picture This" drill, 123
  rogue's gallery of, 119
  solid hit, 118
  Split Grip Energy drill, 127
Drag the Bag drill, 127
Draw
  ball position, 75
  Draw Follow-Through drill, 134
Draw Follow-Through drill, 134
Driver Shadow Practice Line drill, 126
Dynamic balance, 84–85

E
Energy Transfer drill, 124
Extension myth, 30–32

F
Fade
  ball position, 75
  Fade Follow-through drill, 135

Fade Follow-through drill, 135
Fat Shots drill, 153
Finish Flaw drill, 155
Follow-through. *See also* Past Impact to Finish
    symmetrical swing plane, 61
Foot Police drill, 123

G

Gardner Dickinson drill, 120–121
Gentle Elbow Push drill, 125
Grip, 69–73
    grip checks, 69
    grip-friendly helpers, 70
    grip pressure check, 73
    hook-producing chain reaction, 51
    overlap *vs.* interlock, 71
    role of left hand in, 70
    slice-producing chain reaction, 49
    strengthening, 150
    thumb position, 72
    watching your tees and v's, 70

H

Head Movement drill, 152
Head on pillow, 147
Head position
    balanced head, 82
    chin up, 83
    Head Movement drill, 152
    Head on pillow, 147
    keep your head down myth, 26–27
Heel hit, 62–63
Hide the Left Leg drill, 136
Hips
    acceptable body turn, 24
    Push the Right Hip drill, 81
    Regulate Hip Twist drill, 100
Hooks
    hooker's grip, 70
    hook-producing chain reaction, 50–51
    incorrect clubhead position, 47

I

Impact. *See also* Downswing to Impact; Past Impact to Finish; Square at Impact
    degrees off line at, 44
    square at, 6, 141–147
    symmetrical swing plane, 61
Interlock grip check, 71
Iron Shadow drill, 126

J

Johnny Miller Recoil drills, 133–135

K

Keep clubhead low to ground myth, 19–21
Keep Hands Low drill, 94
Keep your head down myth, 26–27

L

Left Arm Check drill, 97
Left arm straight myth, 16–18
Left Hand Over Lap drill, 110

M

Move within the move, 45–51
Myths
    extension myth, 30–32
    keep clubhead low to ground myth, 19–21
    keep your head down myth, 26–27
    left arm straight myth, 16–18
    swing inside to outside myth, 35–37
    swing straight back myth, 28–29
    trapped behind myth, 40–41
    turn, turn, turn myth, 22–25
    weight shift myth, 33–34
    you're swinging over the top myth, 38–39

N

Natural extension, 6
Natural Swing Arc drill, 32
Nerf Ball drill, 101
90-degree backswing rotation, 45, 143

O

180-degree downswing rotation, 46, 143
Overturning, 22–25

P

Parallel-to-the-Target-Line drill, 41
Past Impact to Finish, 129–137
    Anti-Roll drill, 137
    clubhead rotation, 131
    Correctly Finishing the Swing drill, 154
    Draw Follow-Through drill, 134
    Fade Follow-Through drill, 135
    Finish Flaw drill, 155
    Hide the Left Leg drill, 136
    Rotation drill, 132
    Straight Shot Follow-Through drill, 133
    Tee on Left Shoe drill, 137
    three keys for success, 130
"Picture This" drill, 123
Pivot drill #1, 99
Pivot drill #2, 99
Posture, balanced, 77–83
Power punch, 146
Preset Wrist drill, 92
Push the Right Hip drill, 81

R

Regulate Hip Twist drill, 100
Return to the Inside drill, 37
Rhythm, 89
Right and Left Arm Fold drill, 145
Right Elbow in Front of the Body Drill, 105
Right Shoulder Tilt drill, 81
Right Wrist Bend drill, 104

S

Scott McCarron's Balance Beam drill, 77–78
Shadow Coil drill, 102
Shoulders
    acceptable body turn, 24
    chin up, 83
    energize your clubhead, 17
    Head on pillow, 147
    hook-producing chain reaction, 51
    Right Shoulder Tilt drill, 81
    slice-producing chain reaction, 49
Slices
    curing a slice, 150–151
    incorrect clubhead position, 47
    slice-producing chain reaction, 48–49
    slicer's grip, 70
Smooth Acceleration Drill #1: Drop the Ball, 113
Smooth Acceleration Drill #2: Maintain the Tension, 114
Smooth Acceleration Drill #3: Relationship Drill, 115
Split Grip Energy drill, 127
Spokes in wheel, 31
Square at Impact, 137, 141–147
    Head on pillow, 147
    important swing check positions, 142–143
    power punch, 146
    Right and Left Arm Fold drill, 145
    Thumbs Up drill, 144
    270 degrees of rotation, 143

Step-In drill, 112
Still-Head drill, 27
Straight Shot Follow-Through drill, 133
String drill, 18
Sweet spot, 62–63
    Swing Plane Sweet Spot drill, 63
Swing
    extension myth, 30–32
    important swing check positions, 142–143
    incorrect outside-to-inside swing plane, 38
    maintain radius of swing, 20
    misguided distance swing plane misconception, 55
    Parallel-to-the-Target-Line drill, 41
    Return to the Inside drill, 37
    spokes in wheel, 31
    swing goes to low/high misconception, 56–57
    swing inside to outside myth, 35–37
    swing path too high/low, 56–57
    swing too flat misconception, 55
    swing too upright misconception, 54
    symmetrical swing plane, 58–61
    trapped behind myth, 40–41
    Under-the-Noodle drill, 39
    you're swinging over the top myth, 38–39
Swing and Let Go drill, 111
Swing inside to outside myth, 35–37
Swing plane
    incorrect outside-to-inside swing plane, 38
    misguided distance swing plane misconception, 55
    swing inside to outside myth, 36
    Swing Plane drill, 25
    Swing Plane Sweet Spot drill, 63
    Tilted Circle drill, 29
    turn to keep club on plane, 23–25
Swing Plane drill, 25
Swing Plane Sweet Spot drill, 63
Swing straight back myth, 28–29
Symmetrical swing plane, 58–61

T

Takeaway Arm Extension drill, 93
Takeaway drill, 91
Takeaway Slot drill, 95
Tee on Left Shoe drill, 137
Tempo, 89
Tension, 68
Thumbs
    position in grip, 72
    Thumbs Up drill, 144
Thumbs Up drill, 144
Tilted Circle drill, 29

Timing, 89
Toe hit, 62–63
Transition, 107–115
    balanced transition, 108–109
    Left Hand Over Lap drill, 110
    pick the more powerful position, 109
    Smooth Acceleration Drill #1: Drop the Ball, 113
    Smooth Acceleration Drill #2: Maintain the Tension, 114
    Smooth Acceleration Drill #3: Relationship Drill, 115
    Step-In drill, 112
    Swing and Let Go drill, 111
Trapped behind myth, 40–41
Turn, turn, turn myth, 22–25
Turn In the Barrel drill, 98
270 degrees of rotation, 44–51

U

Under-the-Noodle drill, 39

W

Weight shift myth, 33–34
Weight transfer
    Big Punch drill, 34
    weight shift myth, 33–34
Windup Resistance drill, 90

Y

You're swinging over the top myth, 38–39